ENTREPRENEUR
Success
Stories

ENTREPRENEUR
Success
Stories

**How common people
achieve uncommon results**

LORAL LANGEMEIER
AND JOHN C. ROBINSON

LIVEOUTLOUD
CREATING CONVERSATIONS ABOUT MONEY

Entrepreneur Success Stories

How Common People Achieve Uncommon Results

Volume One

Edited by Loral Langemeier and John C. Robinson

Copyright © 2011 Loral Langemeier and John C. Robinson

For information, or to order additional copies of this book, please contact:

Live Out Loud Publishing
Phone: 707-688-2848 | Fax: 707-402-6319
Email: info@earnprofitsfromyourpassion.com

Cover and book design by Cypress House

 is the logo for Live Out Loud Publishing.

LiveOutLoud
CREATING CONVERSATIONS ABOUT MONEY
is the logo for Live Out Loud, Inc., for which Loral Langemeier is Founder and CEO.

Publisher's Cataloging-in-Publication Data

Entrepreneur success stories : how common people achieve uncommon results, volume one / edited by Loral Langemeier and John C. Robinson. -- Marysville, Ohio : Live Out Loud Pub., c2011.
p. ; cm.
ISBN: 978-0-9679338-6-3
1. Entrepreneurship. 2. New business enterprises. 3. Success in business. 4. Business planning. 5. Self-realization.
I. Langemeier, Loral. II. Robinson, John C.,1959-
HB615 .E58 2011 2011915861
658.4/21--dc23 1201

Printed in the USA
1 3 5 7 9 8 6 4 2

Contents

Contents

For Earl M. Cohen,
who encouraged John
to never stop writing

ENTREPRENEUR
SUCCESS
STORIES

INTRODUCTION

Loral Langemeier

ENTREPRENEUR. OF FRENCH ORIGIN; the person responsible for organizing and managing an enterprise, especially a business, and who is accountable for the risks and outcome. It takes considerable initiative to be an entrepreneur.

Economist Joseph Schumpeter once observed that entrepreneurial activities characteristically result in:

+ Innovation

+ Introduction of new technologies

+ Increased efficiency and productivity

+ Generation of new products or services

Examples of great entrepreneurs in history include Benjamin Franklin, Henry Ford, and Thomas Edison. Have you ever wondered if you are an entrepreneur? Likely you have, especially if you are reading this book. And for good reason, as about 465,000 people create new businesses each month in the United States alone*.

One observation I've made over many years is that declaring yourself

---

* Kauffman Index of Entrepreneurial Activity, an annual national assessment performed by the Ewing Marion Kauffman Foundation.

an entrepreneur is a double-edged sword. On the one hand, it gives you great excitement and exhilaration to know you finally have your own business and the ability to create real wealth within your lifetime. On the other hand, many entrepreneurs fall short of their goal because they don't know the first step to take to get started or the repeatable actions necessary to sustain and grow their business.

One dialogue all of us need to enter into more often is about money. Through my company, Live Out Loud, Inc., I provide a forum and suite of programs designed to help individuals, particularly entrepreneurs, discover financial freedom and success. Thousands of people have walked through our doors, and hundreds have gone on to become millionaires.

One program, the Big Table, allows you to join a community of like-minded entrepreneurs for a journey that lasts twelve months and enables you to accelerate the growth of your business. During this program participants meet with me for three two-day sessions and receive private coaching during the remainder of the year from one of our master coaches.

In the past decade I have led more than eighty Big Table sessions. Many graduates of the program have not only achieved uncommon success in their respective businesses, but also return to learn the latest marketing techniques and cutting-edge business-building strategies that are delivered during our annual Big Table alumni community networking events.

Because of the sheer number of clients who have benefited from the Big Table program or who actively practice the entrepreneurial skills we teach, it has always been my dream to capture these successes in one place where they can be shared with a larger audience. John C. Robinson, who is a graduate of Big Table #10, had already published six of his own books and agreed to help by using his publishing company and support team to bring *Entrepreneur Success Stories* to the world stage.

The content on the following pages are part of a larger story that continues to evolve as we proceed toward Big Table #100, and I am proud to share these success stories with you. They will inspire you to greatness and help you reach your full potential.

HOW TO USE THIS BOOK

John C. Robinson and Loral Langemeier

ENTREPRENEUR SUCCESS STORIES is your guiding light to success as an entrepreneur. For a specific need or question, the table of contents will bring you to the very chapter you are looking for. If you have trouble with a legal issue, Richard Banta's "The Entrepreneur and the Law" delivers the most assistance. A month from now you may have trouble believing you can succeed in running a business. That's when you should check out Michelle Prince's "The Power of Belief" to regain your confidence and inspiration.

This book can also be used as a daily learning. Spend thirty minutes with it each day, and read one chapter two or three times to identify the primary message. Ask yourself what you learned from the chapter and how it can be applied to your life or business. There are enough chapters in the book to do this exercise for an entire month.

Over the next thirty days, you will discover how to succeed as a woman in a man's world (see Lorraine Conaway's chapter, "A Woman in a Man's World") or excel in offline marketing (Janet Arline Barker's "Go Where the People Are, Go Where the Money Is"). Shinavi Gupta ("More Passion More Wealth") shows you to put passion into your wealth creation and pave the way to a more fulfilling life.

Others may find their model company in one of these chapters. Loral describes the model company as an individual or business that is already doing what you want to do. Why attempt to grow your business by trial and error, wasting months (if not years) and thousands of dollars in dead-end strategies, when you can model your business after someone who is already playing a bigger and better game? If this scenario describes you, you may spend your time on a single chapter, reading it five or six times, followed by an email to the chapter's writer.

A person who just launched a virtual assistant business will be immediately drawn to Tracie L. Church's chapter, "Get Off Your Hamster Wheel — and Succeed." Katrina Sawa's chapter ("Profit From Your Social Media Marketing by 'Networking'") might be the very initiative you want this year. In "A Story of Success," Will Mattox shows how to attract entrepreneurial opportunity in your life so you never have to work another job again.

Each week someone will find an entirely new method of using *Entrepreneur Success Stories* and we are excited to bring this resource to you. Share your own story of uncommon success and write to us at alumnisuccess@liveoutloud.com. Let us know how you attracted triumphant results in your own business. The journey to entrepreneurial success becomes more exciting with each chapter, and the stories begin on page 25. Note that each contributor's name is provided at the beginning of his or her respective chapter. As mentioned previously, many of the contributors are graduates of Loral's Big Table. These alumni have taken the time to share their expertise with you and we encourage you to learn from the success they've created in their business. The Big Table number that follows their name identifies the graduates, as in John C. Robinson (LBT #10)

While you can jump in and read the individual success stories, start with the exercises found in the beginning chapters. By performing these exercises and gaining familiarity with your own business and aspirations for accomplishment, you have the best possible chance for success.

"I Want That!"

How to Recognize an Entrepreneurial Opportunity and Act On It

John C. Robinson

It starts out innocently. The gem is fleetingly revealed, and only the eye of a seasoned entrepreneur recognizes its value. If not claimed, the fortune disappears just as swiftly, never to be seen again. Here's an example.

"John, what was the date that we saw the American Avocet at Crab Orchard National Wildlife Refuge?" My friend, Todd, was working on an article regarding unusual bird migrants in southern Illinois. He was frantically searching for details regarding an observation he and I had made together at a wildlife refuge more than ten years ago. Both of us were practicing ornithologists in southern Illinois and we had just sat down in my den to discuss his project. While we spoke, I fired up the computer database I had built for myself earlier that year.

In less than forty-five seconds, I had his answer. "Todd, we saw that bird on the ninth of November, 1982," I responded.

There was a long pause in our conversation. Then Todd asked the inevitable question: "John, how can you remember when it happened over a decade ago?"

I told him about my database. He jumped out of his chair and looked over my shoulder at my computer screen. When I showed him all my bird observations for the past fourteen years had already been entered, all he could say was, "Wow."

He challenged me with another observation he and I had made in Williamson County, Illinois, in May 1983. When I pulled up that record in less than fifteen seconds, he demanded, "I want that."

Those were the magic words. It was the first time I contemplated what I had built for my personal use might actually be of value to others. This simple database idea went on to be the flagship product in my business, selling hundreds of thousands of copies worldwide. In fact, Todd was my very first customer.

The success of an entrepreneurial idea will hinge on whether you are able to provide a product or service that solves someone's problem or meets their needs. Moreover, it is common to be unaware what you have created can be sold.

■ RECOGNIZING THE VALUE

FOR SOME INDIVIDUALS, the ability to recognize an entrepreneurial opportunity seems to be instinctive, almost as if they were born with it. If you've never operated a business, you may not have the skill that enables you to instantly spot an entrepreneurial chance of a lifetime. Don't worry if you fall into this category, because the good news is this skill can be learned.

As in the case above, when someone says, "I want that," this is a clear indication to look at what you have and ask why that person became excited over your product or service.

Consumer insight is critical at this stage. Just knowing a consumer wants what you have is not good enough. You must dig deeper and understand the consumer's wants, needs, and pains. In my instance, I could have built an exact replica of my personal bird observation database and placed it on the commercial market. Bad mistake. Be willing to put your ego aside and assume your wants and needs don't exactly mirror those of your customers. What you discover in this part of the process is the many additional features and benefits to include in your product, driving greater consumer demand and increasing sales over time.

In my chapter, "From Concept to Cash," I approached this important aspect of business development by studying my competition and my customer. Identify and address the primary consumer insights during the development phase of your product or service, and you will significantly increase the odds of a successful business launch.

Regardless of whether you are working on your very first product or your fifteenth, always keep a keen eye on the entrepreneurial landscape of your business. Know how to calculate the cost of goods sold, and what the margin is on each of the products or services you offer. One reason to do this is to identify those products that might be ideal for joint venture opportunities or for inclusion in a bundle with one of your existing products. Bundling, by the way, is a great method to strategically package multiple products and increase overall sales relative to when products are sold separately.

Sometimes you introduce a product to your customer database and a buying frenzy ensues. When consumers are ready to fight over your stuff, you know you have a winner. Obviously this doesn't happen frequently, but when it does you need to reposition your new product or service and ride its popularity as you generate waves of sales.

With the advent of digital and information technology, the ability to quickly recognize potential value in the marketplace has never been greater. With one social media post on your Facebook page or blog, you can immediately gauge the response of your audience to a new idea. You can even incorporate their comments, content, and feedback into the actual product before it launches.

The purpose, vision, and values of your business should be clearly identified and shared with everyone on your team. If this has not been done, now is the time to do so. As you develop new products or services, or contemplate new consumer insights, always pass them through the lens of your business' purpose, vision, and values.

As a leader, you need to know when to say, "No." For example, you will inevitably encounter a new business opportunity, product, or business idea that could be added to your sales and marketing funnel. If it is inconsistent with the overall purpose, mission, and values of your business, then move on and look at the next business opportunity instead of wasting your time on an idea that will take you off task. Those who are not willing to adhere to this standard may find that it takes months or even years before they are able to realign their business for strategic growth.

■ PULLING THE TRIGGER

ALL OF US have greatness inside of us. The potential we possess is unlimited, but few of us act on the entrepreneurial impulses that come our way so effortlessly.

You can break yourself of this destructive habit. To start, buy yourself a journal. If you need to put this book down, drive to your local office supply store, and purchase one — do it now. Don't worry. We'll wait until you return.

Got your journal? Your next step is making a record of any entrepreneurial idea that enters your mind, from this day forward. Here is a suggested format for making your journal entries:

Date:
Key consumer insight (what problem the consumer is trying to solve or what need they have):
Core idea for the business opportunity (summarize with as much detail as possible):
Why is this important to your business? (describe relevance to purpose, mission, and vision)
What is the next action you will take to move the business idea forward?
By what date will you take this action?

Recording your big business idea is just the first step. You must be committed to taking action. Here are some ideas:

* Each week talk with a trusted accountability partner and use the time to share your ideas for new business opportunities and/or to build implementation strategies around those opportunities.

* Better yet, use your business team (the people who work on and in your business) to do the same thing. For example, I have a weekly call with my business development team during which time I share the new strategies I have developed and my initial plans for implementing them.

* Share your ideas and thoughts with your business development coach and brainstorm around implementation strategies.

* If you don't yet have a business development coach, get one.

* Once your action plan is in place, be sure to schedule weekly time on your calendar to allow progress to be made on your new business venture.

One of the things that frequently stop us in our tracks is the fear of failure. For others, it is the fear of success. Some of us are afraid to pull the trigger because if our friends, family, and acquaintances know what we are doing, what will they say if we don't succeed? How can we face these people knowing that we fell down?

The secret is to realize failure is inevitable. When you fall down, pick yourself back up. More importantly, remember some of the greatest successes in entrepreneurial history followed one or more failures. You can minimize the number of failures by using a business coach to guide you on your journey. As for those friends, family, and acquaintances: if they don't support you, don't give them power. Aside from your spouse or partner, there is no need to tell them what you are doing. If they are not supportive of what you want to achieve, neutralize that part of the equation by finding new friends, business colleagues, fellow entrepreneurs, or other individuals who have a positive mindset and are willing to help you succeed. Spend time with these people and use their positive energy to encourage your business idea.

Is this easy? At first it might not seem so, and that is why this book was written. *Entrepreneur Success Stories* not only pays tribute to the entrepreneur in all of us, but also serves to highlight the work of Loral Langemeier, who has elevated the potential that entrepreneurs can achieve. Her work is featured throughout the programs she offers at www.liveoutloud.com, most notably in her Big Table program.

Many of the contributors to this book are graduates of Loral's Big Table coaching program. Their essays, alongside other successful entrepreneurs, reveal the secrets to success — told from as many vantage points as possible. The impact the Big Table coaching program has on the acceleration and growth in your business is not overlooked, and many examples in this book explain why.

For those who discover *Entrepreneur Success Stories* as a result of a random search on the Internet or by browsing the retail book shelf, we encourage you to read the exciting ways you can change the results you are getting and achieve success as an entrepreneur. If you are looking for a community of like-minded, positive-thinking entrepreneurs, you will not find a better bunch than the Live Out Loud community.

The following two chapters provide the foundation necessary to get the most out of this book. Read them before the individual stories that follow. The next entrepreneur success story to be told could be yours.

THE ENTREPRENEUR'S BLUEPRINT FOR SUCCESS

John C. Robinson and Loral Langemeier

THAT CREATIVE STREAK in you can't be tamed. Or you want to leave your W-2 job. In some instances, you inherit the opportunity. The reasons to start and run a business are many. What never changes is the quest for success — and especially the questions involving "how."

Loral and I have followed this blueprint for success for many years, and we've boiled it down into a few easy-to-follow steps. Whether you are currently launching a business or have run one for several years, read through this chapter to determine if there are improvements that can be made to your company.

The entrepreneur's blueprint for success consists of the following strategies, systems, and procedures:

1. *Find Your Place on the Map.* Know where you are before you begin your journey. To do this, work with your bookkeeper or accountant to create a profit and loss statement and a balance sheet. Once these are assembled, you will know, on average, how much income you make and how much you spend on a monthly basis. In addition, you will know if your net worth (your assets minus your outstanding liabilities) is positive or negative. Although individual circumstances will vary, a net worth of between $30,000 and $200,000 is not uncommon.

2. *Discover the Gap: Determine What You Want.* Now that you know where you are, it is time to define where you want to go. This is not unlike creating two points on a map and charting a route from the first location to the second. Ask yourself what you really want out of life. Your answers should touch on the four pillars of success: financial, spiritual, health, and family. Define your desired state of existence when success has been acquired by describing the outcomes in these four pivotal areas.

For example, "Twelve months from now, I have a net worth of $700,000 and a monthly net cash flow of $5,000. I live with my husband and two children on a property containing three acres of land, picturesque mountain landscapes in a 360-degree panorama, and located thirty minutes from the beach. While running our international coaching business out of our home, we have time to exercise one hour a day four days each week. Two percent of our net revenue is donated each year to the Missionaries of Charity in the name of Mother Teresa."

If you have trouble stating your financial objective, consider using Loral's Fast Cash Formula: twelve/four/five. Here is how it works:

Twelve — Decide how much money you want to make each month of the year.

Four — Divide that number by the four weeks in a month, to see how much you need to make a week to hit that monthly target.

Five — Divide that number by five working days a week, to see how much you need to make a day to reach that weekly target.

Obviously, this is also an excellent time to identify the core values that define you as a human being. Each person's core values (peace, integrity, innovation, power) are different. What are yours?

3. *Skill Assessment.* Assess the variety of skills you possess. This is done to ensure the Cash Machine (business) you choose or already have is a good match for the skills you possess. Make a list of your key skills.

_____

_____

_____

Don't be afraid to peel back the layers as you do this exercise — this will help define what you are really good at. For example, one client is good at organizing. What are they good at organizing, data or people or something totally different? Organizing data and organizing people are separate skill sets. If you have trouble identifying your skills, ask yourself what are the three most important things you have ever done or created — and what skills enabled you to make those accomplishments.

4. *Choose Your Cash Machine.* Ideally, the business you select is a good fit for your existing skill set and knowledge base. The focus is on enabling you to make cash doing something you already know and/or are skilled at. Many people get stuck at this stage. They are afraid to choose the wrong Cash Machine. There is no right or wrong answer here — this is still the discovery stage. The subsequent steps will help validate your choice of a Cash Machine. Write in the space below the Cash Machine you would like to own and operate:

_____

5. *Leverage the Experience of Three Model Companies.* What most entrepreneurs fail to realize is that someone has already succeeded in doing what they aspire to do. Rather than build your business by trial and error, learn from those who have already paved the way. You can shave months if not years from the time needed to grow your company to the level you desire. There are four ways to learn from the model company:

a. Work for them. Work for a large accounting firm for six to eight months before quitting and use your experience to build your own accounting business modeled after the big firm you have worked for.

b. Interview them. Choose a successful company or individual, and ask for thirty minutes of their time to share their secrets for success. Successful individuals do not live from a mindset of lack and limitation. They see the world as an abundant place and know that sharing some of their success will not have an impact on their own ability to grow and prosper.

c. Become their client. By becoming the customer of your model company, you see their sales process from start to finish. How do they sell to you? What benefits do they invoke to get you to buy? What is their customer service after the sale? Once you become their customer, what else do they try to market to you? Who are they marketing to (target client) and where do they find their target client? What techniques do they use to get their target client to make repeat purchases? What motivates them as a business (what is their purpose and mission)?

d. Spy on them. You can "spy" on your model company with legitimate, publicly available Internet tools. Learn their marketing strategies and identify the key words they use to promote their business. Work with an Internet marketing consultant to gain access to these business development tools.

6. *Revenue Model.* This is the stage where you validate whether the Cash Machine you've chosen can generate the results you want. Before you do that, leverage your interaction with your model company to define the purpose, mission, and values of your business. Your objective is to have your business reflect the uniqueness of you — and distinguish itself from the competition.

a. Purpose. The purpose represents the ultimate intention of your business. It addresses "why" your business exists. For example, "Google, Inc., was founded to make finding high quality information on the web easier and faster." Look at your notes and define the purpose of your business in your own unique way.

b. Mission. On the way to fulfilling your purpose, you can accomplish one or more big initiatives or strategic actions, and these can be summarized into your mission statement. For example, "Through our subsidiaries and nationwide network of distributors, Conseco helps nearly five million customers step up to a better, more secure future. Conseco is a Fortune 500 company, with more than four billion dollars in annual revenues. Our common stock is traded on the New York Stock Exchange under the symbol CNO." How would you define the mission of your business?

c. Values. These encompass your true essence and represent who you are and what you stand for. You have already identified your personal values in a previous exercise. Do you expect your business to reflect those same values? If not, what values would be different?

d. Revenue model. Based on your model company research, you know what products and services you could offer. Take a moment and assign a price to each item. Once this task is completed, create a simple revenue model in an Excel spreadsheet by forecasting your monthly expenses and sales over a twelve- or twenty-four-month period, and sum up your net profit or loss on a monthly basis. This is an iterative process that is repeated several times until you can realize the financial goals identified in step two, "Discover the Gap: Determine What You Want."

7. *Launching the Business.* This involves several activities that must be done on a somewhat parallel timeline: creation of your sales and marketing plan, establishing the business foundation, networking and offline marketing, and identifying the team members who will join you on the path to success. Let's touch on each of these.

a. Sales and marketing plan. Write down the top three benefits for each of your products and services. Next, list the top three problems, needs, or wants your target market has. Use these two lists to practice your speech on how to position your business in front of your customer to solve their problems.

The goal of this exercise is to define your marketing message. Your marketing message will have more relevance to your customers if you have a defined market niche. To build your marketing message, start with an elevator speech, which is an abbreviated synopsis (fifteen seconds or less) that explains what you do and piques your prospect's interest. For example, John's elevator speech is, "I help entrepreneurial authors and creators of information products unlock the hidden sources of income in their business."

Once completed, your sales and marketing plan defines your business goals, the strategies or methods to reach those goals, and the specific tactics or actions to take. While it is feasible to build this plan on your own, you'll find it much more productive and efficient to hire a professional business-plan writer.

b. Establish the business foundation. Your business foundation includes activities that range from ongoing research and corporate entity creation to the opening of your bank account, procurement of a business license, and the establishment of your website and accompanying merchant account. Fortunately, there are specialists who can streamline most of this work for you. While this might not be the most glamorous part of being in business, the paperwork keeps the doors to your business open and free from trouble.

c. Networking and offline marketing. While your sales and marketing plan are built and your business is created, many entrepreneurs believe that everything must be perfect before they can ask for the cash. This mistake can be avoided by committing to a regimen of networking and offline marketing. As an example, one client decided to be a handyman. Within two weeks of that decision, he made his first thousand dollars. How did he do it? By getting out in his local community, talking to people using his elevator speech and key benefit statements, and not being afraid to ask for the cash. He went on to make a minimum of $4000 each month for the remaining time he was in Loral's coaching program. What networking and offline marketing strategy will you commit to?

_____

_____

_____

d. Identifying the team. In order to find entrepreneurial success, your business needs to be supported by a team of key individuals. Some of these people, such as bookkeepers, personal or virtual assistants, web designers, and copywriters, will work in your business. Other individuals (attorneys, coaches, financial advisers) work on your business. Who will be on your team, and when do you plan to bring them on board?

_____

_____

_____

8. *Expanded Growth and Acceleration.* At this point in the entrepreneur's blueprint, you are poised for unlimited success. When your website comes online, you are ready to leverage affiliate and other online marketing techniques, entertain joint venture opportunities, and launch a series of targeted marketing campaigns designed to promote one or more of your products and services. This enables you to achieve expanded growth and acceleration in your business. The success of your business is determined by how well you understood and replicated your business model.

This blueprint is provided to help you understand the process necessary to start and grow any business. Obviously, space limits how much detail can be provided for each step, but the stories later in this book will show you how to leverage the output you created using the blueprint for your own entrepreneurial success story.

Of Gremlins and Saboteurs

The Battle on the Path to Success

John C. Robinson and Loral Langemeier

Have you given birth to a gremlin or saboteur? The symptoms are easy to recognize: procrastination, low self-esteem, lack of belief, or no self-confidence. Some of us have a whole family of these mental offspring, having delivered twins, triplets, or quadruplets. The worst part about it is — they never seem to grow up and leave home.

John's friend, Todd, helped him discover the kernel of an entrepreneurial idea for a multimedia software program that could be marketed and sold worldwide. The business went on to become very successful and thrives to this day. Now it's time for the rest of the story.

While still in college, John took a computer-programming course in FORTRAN. Although he passed the course with a B average, he remembered it as being one of the most difficult classes he took. At the end of the semester he swore he would never be good at computer programming. With that single thought, a saboteur was born.

This little gremlin traveled with John for over a decade, growing stronger with each reinforcing thought. He was there when John purchased his first PC in 1986, and laughed out loud when John installed his first database program on that computer in 1987. The laughs turned into jeering taunts and maniacal howls when John upgraded his information management system to an Oracle relational database in 1992.

Imagine the vicious attack that took place in the fall of 1993 when the idea first surfaced in John's mind that he could develop a computer program and sell it to a global audience. "You are NOT a computer programmer," the gremlin scolded.

It would have been so easy to quit right there. After all, John had spent over twelve years telling himself that writing computer programming code was something he would never be able to learn. The gremlin became even more animated when John purchased his first book on computer programming in October 1993. "John, what are you doing? Don't you know how futile this will be?" The gremlin's spears were sharp to the touch.

The battle raged for several days. The skirmishes were many, but in the end John won. He did it by practicing two mental strategies:

◆ Follow your passion.

◆ Be persistent in everything you strive to achieve.

■ FOLLOW YOUR PASSION

NAPOLEON HILL ONCE wrote, "Cherish your visions and your dreams, as they are the children of your soul, the blueprints of your ultimate achievements." What are your visions and dreams? Take a moment to write them down:

_____

_____

_____

If you let go of your visions and dreams, you forego the opportunity to reach your greatest achievements. All too often, people spend forty, fifty, or even sixty hours a week laboring at something they are not passionate about. We give you permission to dream again — to pursue the thoughts and ideas that have always excited you.

We realize you have to make money and how you do that may not necessarily fuel your passion. That's okay so long as you decide what you really want, set a date when you intend to acquire it, and build a plan to attract what is yours. Using this strategy your passion will never become lost. By setting a date for when you intend to achieve your goal and possess the lifestyle you've always wanted, you can back into a plan that will get you there.

How is this done? First, be very specific in describing the goal or goals you want to achieve. Don't say, "I'm going to invest in real estate and make lots of money." This statement does not commit you to any path of fruitful action.

Instead, state your goal like this: "I'm going to invest in real estate by purchasing three single-family residence homes in San Antonio, Texas. I will purchase my first two homes by November of this year and the third property by April of next year, using a local team that I will have in place by September 30. Within thirty days of closing on each property, I will have a tenant in each home, and the net profit from the monthly rent paid by the tenant will be $165." Notice how SMART goals are used to describe what you want. Each letter in the word SMART stands for an attribute of your goal or goals:

- "S" means the goal is *specific* (going to San Antonio, Texas and purchase only single-family residence homes using a local team).

- "M" means *measurable*. In this case, purchase three properties and intend to have a net profit of $165 per month per property.

- "A" means *achievable*. Your ability to accomplish something increases when you surround yourself with a team versus doing all the work yourself. With the collective skills, strengths, and weaknesses of the team surrounding you, a goal is achievable.

- "R" means *realistic*. This means the goal can be achieved in the timeframe you have set.

- ◆ "T" means *timely*. Time-bound goals are the best because you have created a sense of urgency to hit your milestones.

Once your goals are defined, you can back into a plan of action. For example, let's say you have used the SMART concept to fully describe one or more goals you want to achieve in twelve months. To back into your plan, where do you need to be in six months so you are on track to hit your one-year goal or goals? Once you visualize and describe this milestone, then there is only one question left: What do I need to do over the next 120 days to hit my six-month milestone?

Every student who has joined Loral's Big Table or Wealth Acceleration programs is familiar with the 120-day plan. It is a tool of the wealthy, which is why you need to create one as well.

The plan takes the major tasks that need to be done (hiring an attorney or setting up an entity) and breaks them down into individual action items. For example, to set up an entity, you may need to:

1. Decide on a name for your business entity (e.g., ABC Consulting, LLC).

2. Complete the paperwork for setting up the entity.

3. Decide on which bank you will use to open the business' checking and savings accounts.

4. Set up the bank accounts.

5. Complete corporate minutes as needed.

For each action, identify when they are initiated and when they are completed, and by whom. Your 120-day plan is most valuable when you share it with your coach or mastermind team and use them to hold you accountable.

▩ BE PERSISTENT

WITHOUT A DOUBT, persistence will enable you to achieve more than you ever thought possible. Napoleon Hill described persistence as "the sustained effort necessary to induce faith" and identified it as one of the thirteen steps necessary to achieve wealth.

The gremlins and saboteurs that strive to keep us from our goals are all around us. They can be friends, family, or even us. On your journey toward success and greater achievement, these demons will remind you that everything you attempt to do is in vain, it won't work, and it is fruitless to try. The first time you make a mistake or have a loss in your business, they are quick to point out their predictions have come true. They will challenge you to justify why you would continue in the face of such seemingly overwhelming odds.

Many times the gremlins win. Imagine what might happen if you were able to push past the negative thoughts and negative energy that is constantly thrown at you by the saboteurs you let into your life. The mind is a powerful thing, and you need to let it unleash its full power in support of you. The thrill of having a breakthrough moment in the middle of a major product launch or during the development phase of a new innovation cannot be described — the satisfaction, confidence, and accomplishment must be experienced firsthand.

In these chapters are the tools you need to be persistent for your own entrepreneurial success: the purpose and mission of your business, defining what you want and capturing that desire in writing, and building strategic plans based on one or more model companies. The rest is up to you. You must concentrate and direct your mind, energy, and thoughts toward the attainment of your goals and satisfy the desire that is deep within you.

Everyone differs in their ability to rely on themselves for implementing a regimen of persistence. While some can adopt this behavior more easily than others, everyone can learn this skill and become better at it. The key is to build a plan and follow it persistently. Along the way, you can leverage the resources, experiences, and power of others as needed.

Following are twenty-eight stories of entrepreneurial success. Each of the contributors practiced some form of persistence to achieve their results. As you read the chapters, ask what you can learn from their persistence — and how you can apply the same level of tenacity to your own entrepreneurial endeavors.

But most importantly, remember the tale of the saboteur. This tale is so important, Loral and I have highlighted it in more detail (see Jeannette McCarroll's chapter, "The Saboteur: The Most Powerful of Thieves").

The Entrepreneur and the Law

Richard Banta (LBT #5)

My wife Theresa and I have created uncommon results using the Live Out Loud wealth building strategies. Our experience is that long-term success is not a sprint or a question of how fast you reach your goal. It is a measured, thought-out, well-planned process. Right now you might say to yourself, "I want in. How do I get started?" Simple. You make a decision and start right where you are.

I met Loral in 2003 when her Big Table program and the Live Out Loud community were just getting started. I am an attorney with my own practice, and an entrepreneur. I liked Loral's message and my intuition told me that joining her Big Table would be wise. In June of 2003 I met the members of Big Table #1 when they had their third session in Denver. I liked the conversation. Next thing I knew it was August and I was heading to San Mateo, California for Big Table #5. Theresa later joined Big Table #8. Joining the Big Table and the Live Out Loud community is one of the best decisions I've made.

When I joined Loral's Big Table I was less than focused on creating wealth. I live in Colorado and building wealth was not a priority. Skiing, white water rafting, and spending as much time as possible outdoors consumed most of my time outside of my law practice. I get being an entrepreneur. I've worked for myself most of my life. It was the wealth building piece that I was short on, and the importance of team. Even though Theresa and I were happy, there was this small voice in the back of my head saying, "You should be paying more attention to your finances. Doesn't have to be a big move to start, something simple like balancing your checkbook."

Since that time, we moved from our home of eighteen years into a Victorian house which is now our home and place of business. The result is we no longer pay a mortgage along with rent for office space. We have started several businesses and invested in real estate, moving from single-family rentals to purchasing and renovating a large apartment building. Until recently we have doubled our net worth each year using the Live Out Loud wealth building strategies. Once the tremors in the current economy have settled down the opportunities for entrepreneurs — people like you — in the new economy will be enormous. The new economy will be safer, saner, and friendlier to the small business than ever before. It will be fertile ground for common people to create uncommon results.

The Live Out Loud model for building wealth is very precise, but it is not a template. There is no such thing as a template for being an entrepreneur. There are wealth-building strategies. These include writing out goals; developing a written plan; creating a support team (especially a mastermind team); working with a coach; and most importantly, getting into action. This dynamic and fluid model changes as you advance your goals. I like the expression, "goals in concrete, plans in sand." Theresa and I have applied this system to build our wealth. We are always on the lookout for entrepreneurial opportunities.

▮ You've Been Served

When John C. Robinson called me to ask if I would write a chapter, I took it as an omen that I should add my voice to this important conversation. I have written a book on entrepreneurs and the law titled *You've Been Served! The Street Smart Entrepreneurs Guide to the Law: How the Law Works and Why You Need to Know It*. The book should be the first member of your legal team. The book is full of legal forms, frequently asked questions, interview questions for retaining an attorney, anecdotes, jokes, stories, and more. It is a tool for the street-smart entrepreneur to have in his or her library. Armed with the information in the book, entrepreneurs will be empowered to not only lead their legal team but to use the law as a wealth-building tool.

The new "Entrepreneur and the Law" business I am building uses the Live Out Loud wealth strategies. The book explains how the legal system works in plain English. What happens if you get served with a summons and complaint? Are you out of business? Is your bank account going to be closed? Are you headed to the Big House? The book answers these and many other questions. It explains how both the civil and criminal laws work, and will help build an entrepreneur's confidence. Armed with their newfound understanding of the law, an entrepreneur can confidently set up shop knowing the law has their back.

Now, I did not just get up one morning and start writing. I first had to overcome a limiting belief that "It has all been said before." I was working with a coach and during one call the topic of writing a book came up. I gave my standard reply of "It's all been said before." But my coach said to me, "You haven't yet put your voice into the conversation, and if you are going to be true to your life purpose, you owe it to the world to do so." This got me thinking in a whole new and exciting way. It shifted my beliefs dramatically. I realized that I could use my skills as an experienced attorney and entrepreneur to write a book that takes the mystery out of the law and empowers entrepreneurs to lead their legal team.

Once the decision was made, the rest of the project fell into place. I have a specific goal, the book, with a projected publication date of December 2011. I have a written plan, which includes two hours a day of writing and research. I have a coach. I have a mastermind team. What remains is to be consistent to my goal and plan, and persevere in the face of any obstacles that come up. To help overcome those obstacles I keep on my desk a quote from Napoleon Hill's classic book, *Law of Success:* "What helped you over the great obstacles of life?" was asked of a highly successful man. "Why, the other obstacles," he replied.

The questions you should ask yourself are, "Am I an entrepreneur? Do I have what it takes?" The answer is a resounding yes. You can be a successful entrepreneur and the Live Out Loud community will support you in your decision.

■ *Meet the Contributor*

RICHARD BANTA IS a nationally recognized authority on entrepreneurs and the law. He is an honors graduate of George Washington University Law School and also holds a Master of Laws degree from the London School of Economics and Political Science. He is an AV rated attorney by Martindale-Hubbell, and has been listed in the Bar Register of Preeminent Lawyers in America. He is also an entrepreneur in his own right having earned his degree in entrepreneurialism out on the street, and the author of *You've Been Served! The Street Smart Entrepreneurs Guide to the Law: How the Law Works and Why You Need to Know It.* He is active with his wife, Theresa, in the Live Out Loud community where he oversees the mastermind program for Loral's Big Table.

Contact Richard at www.richardbantalaw.com

Mountains High, Rivers Deep

Nick's Seven-Point Survival Guide for Business Owners

Nick Lawler (LBT #60)

The great mountain itself, standing majestic against a cloudless sky, struck awe into the hearts of the puny creatures who were soon to set presumptuous foot on those dreadful slopes. What pen could describe our feelings as we viewed the Rum Doodle massif from the summit of the Rankling La?
— W. E. Bowman, *The Ascent of Rum Doodle*

BEING IN BUSINESS can feel like climbing a mountain. It's easy to lose your way, you can fall off, and getting to the top can be challenging. Success in business though feels like nothing else — apart from standing on top of that mountain. It is realizing our dreams that keep us moving upward whether you are climbing a mountain or building your own business.

But the burden of being responsible for a small business rapidly going under is like drowning in a swirling, fast-moving deep river. Escape seems impossible. I've had both experiences and I'd rather be climbing the mountain any day.

▧ RUNNING A RESTAURANT? YOU MUST BE MAD!

I AM NOT an adrenaline junkie but my driving force has always been for a life filled with excitement and adventure. As an overgrown English schoolboy who dreamed of climbing El Capitan and Alpine north faces, I grew into a classic jaded mid-career wage slave as marriage, mortgages, and children slowly eroded my adolescent dreams. The unhappiness that ensued pushed me to launching a completely new endeavor of running a small hotel and restaurant.

Do you know what the failure rate is among start-up restaurants? Well, no. I missed that piece of research, though with the benefit of hindsight, some research and soul-searching might have been a good thing. With the support of my wife (our two children were toddlers and mostly compliant), we found a dreamy historic manor house off the beaten track, nestled in the prettiest valley in the English Lake District, a popular tourism destination outside of London. Any half-scribbled business plan that may have existed was discarded. We were buying into an escape, a dream, and a lifestyle. Running a viable business was not something either of us worried about. A few vaguely stated affirmations, and the job was done.

You might love hotels and restaurants but have no intention of running your own business. Sensible people know that a work/life balance can't be achieved in a seven-day-a-week job with built-in unsocial hours. I might persuade you into believing the hospitality industry, including the transient nature of its customers, is sexy and glamorous, or that it is the location of romantic engagements and consequent couplings. I definitely sign up to that: romantic candlelit meals, first dates, engagements, weddings, christenings, and anniversaries are the things I most love when I'm at work. I rarely get invited but I'm often there, and being part of our guests' significant life events and helping craft the treasured memories is still my passion.

"Would it go?"
— from *The Ascent of Rum Doodle*

THE GREAT QUESTION was: will it go? Well, nine years later and I have been up the mountain and in the swirling river. My initial energy and enthusiasm was strong enough to see me half-way up the mountain (by which time sixty percent of new restaurants have failed) but there wasn't enough chocolate in my rucksack to keep me going and I found myself back in the valley accidentally falling in the river. I grabbed a few branches on my way downstream but they broke and I continued toward the waterfall.

Fate intervened (or maybe this river trip was not survivable without help) and a fairy-tale princess rescued me. I wish that was true. She turned out to be an arse-kicking cowgirl who threw me a lasso for my credit card, and a second lasso to drag me out of the river when my money had cleared. Loral dried me out by slow roasting over her cowgirl campfire and made me chew some beans.

Over several trips to her mountain home I learned to refill my rucksack with food, though this time it was a more balanced menu including lots of protein, and she gave me a guide and a map before putting me back on my own mountain.

The second time up the mountain has been more fun, with the summit clearly in sight. My map has stopped me from getting lost and given me time to reflect on how close I came to disaster.

After some early success and small profits in the first three years of the business, I ran out of steam:

+ I had manifested my goal: to run a lifestyle business. It was just that my business was my lifestyle and left no room or energy for anything else, least of all family, friends, and my own health.

+ There were some weird paradigms going on in my head about money and wealth that pre-dated me trying to run my own business.

+ I didn't value (or spend time) on the finances of the business — see note above.

+ I grew a business based on turnover, not learning the important lesson that turnover equals vanity, profit equals sanity, and cash equals reality.

+ I allowed accountants who didn't understand my business to determine how my profit and loss account should be structured, thus making it hard for me to work out my actual fixed and variable costs.

Recovering from the shock of it all, I've learned some valuable lessons. Here is my seven-point survival guide for anyone thinking about buying your own hotel or restaurant (but equally applicable to other businesses).

The first is: It's bloody easy to get yourself into a terrible mess.

The second is: Start with your money eyes wide-open.

My wife, Ann, and I were incredibly naive. Like most households we were good at watching the pennies but useless at managing the pounds. We could tell you how much we spent at the supermarket each week, but we committed to the largest financial investment of our lives without a second thought.

Ask yourself these questions:

+ How much time do I spend managing the grocery bill?

- How much time do I spend managing my credit card debt?

- How much time do I spend evaluating the financial consequences of buying a house?

If you find yourself a bit disappointed with the answers, don't worry — you are normal. But if you dream of running your own business one day, develop your financial muscle now and exercise some due diligence on this pipe-dream before you go any further.

Consultants always flog their services and I am increasingly struck by the need to be more business-minded right from the start — we were not. So this is what I recommend: Spend some money up front and commission a market study before you begin.

The third lesson is: Make sure you have plenty of spare cash or an adequate loan facility to buy the extras.

We had so much stuff break down in the first twenty-four months. Everything in the kitchen had reached the end of its useful life and broke down together. Also, if your business is property-based, you want to make the place your own and that means spending money. You should spend the money because you can't help but show pride when you are happy with your offering. It also shows when you are not happy. So you will end up spending more money than you budgeted for, and you need cash to market your services to a new or wider pool of potential customers.

The fourth lesson is: Don't expect a nine-to-five life.

I'm pretty carefree, fun and outgoing, enjoying the company of strangers, and capable of talking to anyone who stands still long enough. I'm also a workaholic and only occasionally miss having a normal weekend. A good friend recently slipped me a questionnaire and I was quite pleased to score nineteen out of twenty. I was less pleased to discover it was the Workaholics Anonymous questionnaire.

My best work (always has been and always will be) takes place between the hours of 11 p.m. and 2 a.m., so don't talk to me before 11 a.m. In many ways I am ideally suited to life as an hotelier. Are you?

If things start to go wrong, the fifth lesson is: It will take time to turn things around.

This is particularly true if you are not prepared to take a hatchet to the entire business. If you are flailing helplessly in the water, you won't understand how your business is structured and how to reduce your costs and increase your profitability quickly. You need to learn some lessons.

The sixth lesson is: Write out your organizational structure, put it in a drawer, refer to it regularly, and start putting the people in place.

If you are trying to grow a business based on a team (every restaurant needs its chefs and every hotel needs its housekeepers), write out your ideal structure and fill in the gaps. Don't make my mistake and penny-pinch by putting more people in at the bottom. My business started to accelerate the second time around when I invested in a business partner that shared the dream and responsibility, and gave us some management clout to turn our vision into reality. Trying to grow additional revenue streams without a management team in place to deliver the extra service required is a sure way to an early grave. You just can't manage it all.

The seventh and final lesson is: Be focused and optimistic about your future and the vision you have for your business.

It is the only way to have enough energy to get you out of bed each day and keep your business moving forward. If this means investing in yourself, giving you the skills, strategies, and mindset of entrepreneurs, do it as your number one priority.

If you want to survive, take your team and your customers with you. Slumping into depression doesn't help. I know. I tried it.

That finishes the whirlwind tour of my first nine years in business. Somehow my marriage survived the ups and downs of our business in the mountains and we managed to add a third baby to our tribe. I'm now a recovering workaholic that enjoys the benefits of living in a beautiful part of the world, surrounded by the mountains I love, as well as my family and their animals; cats, chickens, dogs, fish, gerbils, guinea pigs, horses, and pigs. Nothing gives me more pleasure than coming home from work to find the family in our fields with the animals and the backdrop of mountain scenery. I'm looking forward to the next nine years, as long as it doesn't involve more animals.

▨ *Meet the Contributor*

NICK LAWLER is the owner of Winder Hall, a hotel and restaurant in the English Lake District, the number-one tourism destination outside of London, UK. Winder Hall also provides outside catering, conference, event, and wedding services. As the co-founder and Chief Development Officer of All Systems Go Now (ASGN) Hospitality, based in Portland, Oregon, Nick splits his time between the UK and USA. ASGN provides training and private client services to hotel and restaurant business owners who believe in the unreasonable pursuit of perfect hospitality and want superior systems to reduce costs and increase profitability.

Contact Nick at www.asgnhospitality.com

A Story of Success

Will Mattox

THE TRUTH IS I am not employee material and I know that I never have been. I was the one who had a better way, and became bored with taking direction from others or helping achieve somebody else's agenda.

My last job was selling shoes as I completed high school in Phoenix, Arizona over forty years ago. What started out as a summer job became a part-time gig during my senior year and I excelled because of a natural gift of gab and an immediate recognition that selling is a game, almost a contest, between seller and buyer. The game aspect made it bearable and I was quickly the top sales person for a large chain of stores. You might think I wanted to ride that success and stay in sales, but I found myself surrounded by idiots and I couldn't wait to get out of there and on with my real life, whatever that was to be.

I never set out to become an entrepreneur and spent four years of college on an art education degree — do you know how little an art teacher makes?

Life has a way of giving us what we expect or what we believe we are entitled to receive. I believed it was going to be an Ozzie and Harriet life generously sprinkled with freedom and creativity. I put myself through school by making pottery and planned to go to graduate school in Oregon as part of the hippie lifestyle that was so popular. Life stepped in and closed the door to grad school and opened the door to poverty and challenge. When was Ozzie going to show up?

Living in our VW bus, my wife of two years and I had almost no money, no job, no apparent future, and yet were excited about our prospects (no, we were not doing drugs). I started making pottery again and happened to be in the right place at the right time with the opening of the first Saturday market in the United States in 1971. Success was ours. Thirty years later I retired as one of the most successful and largest pottery producers in the Northwest. I expected to be successful and always said I would retire before I was fifty; at forty-seven years old I was again ready to move on to what's next.

It turns out that what's next isn't always readily apparent. I had invested in real estate a little and designed and built a mini-storage project that became our primary revenue stream with about four hours a month of required oversight. Most of you reading this would think that is pretty wonderful, but I became bored with the retired lifestyle — reading, golf, vacations — and started looking for the next challenge.

I expected to find another avenue to fulfillment, and that led to opportunity. An opportunity will show up, sometimes many, to allow us to achieve our expectations. The hard part is that we have to act quickly before they pass by. In my case, action required me to go back to school to try this new thing called life coaching. My only prior experience with coaching involved sports and I wasn't excited about that. Life coaching was the dream of many people who wanted to wear their pajamas all day and be paid to talk to people on the telephone. This sounded good to me.

After two years of training and school I was ready to impart my wisdom to any and all that paid me. Again I met with poverty and challenge and the need to work to achieve success.

The first thing that every coaching client asks for help with is making more money in the belief that any problem is solved with cash. However, the one aspect of coach training that was never discussed was the business of making more money, for me or for my clients. Luckily I had thirty years of business success to fall back on.

At the Coaches Training Institute in California, I met Loral Langemeier. She was a kindred spirit that recognized the gaping hole in coaching because it did not address the first request of all clients for more money. Her business and corporate background and my entrepreneurial business background set us apart from the crowd. As we looked at market differentiation we knew we had something others did not: successful experience. Call it "expertise" — it is a commodity with trading power.

Loral and I started working and investing together. We created financial and business coaching programs and were ready to take on the world, but once again we were met with poverty and challenge. We knew we were onto something, and Loral announced it was time to write books, be on stages, and travel the world with a new company called "Live Out Loud." I, too, wanted to start a new company, called "Live Quietly and Leave Me Alone." I was already financially comfortable and did not want the twenty-four hours a day, seven days a week lifestyle she described. That led to my working as the coach trainer with Live Out Loud and the only alumni coach, which is where my passion has always been: helping others find their path to success, and understanding business, marketing, and financial principles. Being a part of my clients' success is still hugely rewarding.

Having now worked with and coached thousands of people, I find that the keys to their success are the same as they were for me. There are some very simple principles that almost assure success as an entrepreneur. First, you must:

- Know how to attract and recognize opportunity
- Be willing to work hard in the beginning
- Be able to think creatively to differentiate yourself
- Success depends on your ability to make the right decisions
- Be able to take the lead and ask for help

If you don't have these qualities, hire them or partner with others to attain them. I always was blessed with a creative mind and willingness to work hard, but some of the others came through trial and error. Most people do not have both left and right brain styles of thinking, and so decision-making comes hard from just one hemisphere. It is critical to recognize your shortcomings and then fill in the weak areas. Once you have the qualities above, business is simple application and the fundamentals are also relatively simple. For example, all business is supply and demand (sales and delivery). It does not matter if it is product or service based; most problems arise because one side of the equation is missing. When you solve the deficiency, the business will grow. For most of my coaching clients, sales in the current economy are the first place to start — because without sales you don't have a business. You only have an idea that may or may not have the potential to become a successful business. This is an over simplification as what a coach does to fix what's broken is very often a challenging puzzle, but there is no rocket science involved.

Recently I have come to appreciate what I call the next level of understanding of business and even life itself. Everything has three aspects: physical, mental, and spiritual. That means your business, relationships, and personal lives have these aspects and if you want total health in your business you must address all three. If you want total health in your relationships, address all three aspects, and so on. Many of us fail to recognize this basic concept so we work on the physical aspects of our business and ignore the rest, believing if we do the right things in business we will have success; ultimately the business will fail because we've not addressed the mental health and spiritual aspects of our business.

I have become the "Ozzie." I am blessed with a wonderful wife and three successful happy children and now grandchildren. I spend winter in Mexico near the beach, and have time for my real estate projects and continue to coach people around the globe. Years ago, I started with a few simple skills and ideas and have been given more as life challenged me through the coaching clients that I have had the pleasure of working with over the last fifteen years. I learned how to attract opportunity and am better at decision-making, and living the life I envisioned. I have received what I expected.

I love coaching. I love being a part of my clients' success and a member of that lifelong-learning club. Should I have a chance to help you and your business grow as your coach, I guarantee we will both go away changed.

▨ *Meet the Contributor*

WILL MATTOX, CPPC, has over 40 years of entrepreneurial experience, coupled with an education degree and international certification as a business coach. This gives Will the ability to work with clients in a very direct and honest process to create accelerated growth toward their goals. On coaching, he says, "I love being a part of other peoples' success and feeling that I contributed in a positive way." Will is a leader in the coaching profession because he shares his business success in manufacturing, construction, real estate, retail, sales, and coaching, combined with his intuitive ability to get results quickly.

Will and his wife, Virginia, split their time between Lake Oswego, Oregon and Bucerias, Mexico where they recently built a house near the beach and do property development and land sales.

Currently, Will is Owner Operator of "Coaching Services.com" where he works with entrepreneurial clients from around the world in business startup, acceleration, and profitability. He is also Founder and Owner of "Select Mexico Properties.com" (established in 2006 to sell real estate in Mexican Development projects); Owner, Designer, and Contractor for "Storage Parks, Inc.", which operates the Storage Junction mini-storage site in Lane County, OR; and Founder and Owner of "Real Estate Resource Group, LLC", which operates as the real estate acquisition and operation entity for Mattox Properties.

Contact Will at www.coachingservices.com

A Seriously Twisted Tale

The Rise and Fall and Recovery of Our Jewellery Business

Manuela Rocker and Megan Wisheart (LBT #74)

We met at the Manly Art and Crafts Market on Sydney's northern beaches in 2003. We were both selling our own jewellery, and initially wary of whether we would be competing for the same customers. But once we started chatting, we instantly clicked and soon realized we had two very distinctive ranges that complemented each other nicely.

We had the same idea about how to move forward and decided to work together. We came to the Manly market to test our products in every possible way, from design and quality through to pricing. Our intention was to start exhibiting at trade fairs around the country, and then supply retailers. We had great products with real potential but we needed to find out how to get them out there. Our goal was to have a jewellery import/wholesale and manufacturing business. We thrived at the Manly market and by mid 2004 we had our ranges at several other markets and also hired staff.

The income generated from the markets allowed us to book into the first Gift and Homeware Fair in Sydney in September 2004. It was a considerable risk for us at a cost of $7000 plus stock, along with the hours to set up and attend the fair. However, we were blown away by the response we received at the fair and soon realized we needed to make serious changes in our set-up to cope with this new demand. We moved our two home-based businesses into a small premises, and set ourselves up as a company. This is when Seriously Twisted Jewellery Pty Ltd was born. One of our goals was to source the beautiful jewellery from overseas and import it into Australia, and we soon started our hunt for the perfect item.

We fell in love with a new bead and bracelet system from a brand that had just entered Australia and each bought a bracelet with a few beads to slide on. We believed this jewellery would be very popular here as people could personalize their bracelets. At the same time, a Queensland company who liked our jewellery range and presence at trade fairs approached us to represent their jewellery from New South Wales. To our surprise, their jewellery was the same product we loved and had just bought. We immediately accepted the offer and took on the agency for New South Wales. As an added bonus, they told us this range was made in Italy. As Manuela grew up in Switzerland and speaks fluent Italian, this seemed a perfect start to our overseas involvement.

The range was soon doing really well and six months later we became the distributors Australia-wide. One of the strongest selling points for retailers and their customers was that it was "Made in Italy." However, after a few months, we had our suspicions and we discovered we had been lied to and that the range was made in Asia. We were hugely disappointed, not so much because the range was made in Asia but because we had unwittingly lied to our customers.

■ THE RISE — 2005

INTERNET RESEARCH ALLOWED us to find a manufacturer in Tuscany, Italy, that also produced a similar range of jewellery. After a short negotiation, we were given the exclusive Australian distributorship of this new genuine Italian range and started importing immediately.

Truth be told, we were on a high and failed to carry out our due diligence. We started the new relationship without a signed agreement, and this left us open to potential disaster.

However, we were happy with the range: it really took off in Australia, mainly due to the leading brand that I shall not name. Life was good and to add to it, Megan had a girl named Niki in May 2006 while Manuela had a boy named Jett in September of the same year. Yes, life was great.

From the new range our company went from turning over $100,000 per year to turning over more than $2,000,000. We worked hard and put in long hours, while we enjoyed our success and the results that came with it. Everybody loved the jewellery and customers lined up at trade fairs to place orders. We didn't go out and look for new customers; they came to us. The feeling was unbelievable and people in the industry knew and respected us. We supplied over 200 stores in Australia and also entered the New Zealand market. We were the number one distributor in the world for the brand, and distributors from other countries looked up to us.

As much as we were thrilled about the results, our inexperience shone through in many different areas.

■ THE FALL — 2009

ON PAPER OUR company was doing extremely well. We were making a name for ourselves, and enjoying our success. However, we made crucial mistakes that led to infinite discussions and sleepless nights as a consequence. The support from the Italian company was non-existent and we voluntarily took on many extra tasks to make this work.

Two of our biggest problems were communication and the time difference between Italy and Australia. Manuela's native language being Italian solved the first problem (although it created extra work in translation for the rest of our team), but the time difference meant a lot of the dealings were done at night. The other major problem was that the Italian manufacturer pretty much neglected all marketing efforts. There were no catalogues, photographs, or flyers. Megan's background is graphic design, so once again our team took on more work. Megan created flyers, wish lists, special occasion marketing visuals, and many more things besides.

Our main mistakes were:

- Starting a distributorship without a proper contract/agreement and exit strategy.

- Basing our pricing on the main competitor without considering the consequences.

- Starting to look after all the marketing ourselves, and sharing it with other distributors around the world without charging them a dime.

- Encroaching on our family time by spending far too much time working at night to accommodate the Italians.

- Failing to put our foot down and achieve an agreement that suited the manufacturer and us in order to keep growing the brand. There were quality issues and unacceptable delays in the deliveries.

▮ THE SOLUTION

AT THE END of 2009 we met with our accountant and lawyer separately to discuss the situation and for some constructive criticism and advice. We knew it was coming, and the message was clear: Cut your losses and abandon ship at once.

We took time to think this through and made further attempts with the Italians to find a workable solution. Since we started working with them in 2005, the company had changed hands three times and every change involved Italian style drama, complete with car chases, unauthorized entry into a hotel room, and removal of samples concealed in high boots (not kidding).

Early in 2010, we knew it was time for us to move forward and we attended a free ninety-minute presentation given by a leading money expert. Loral Langemeier and her passion for helping and encouraging entrepreneurs (which we always considered ourselves) were just infectious.

We made the decision to relinquish the distributorship and were in a battle with the manufacturer. Luckily for us we had documented events properly and they had nothing on us. Still, this meant there was no chance they would help us find another distributor for Australia or sell the existing stock. We had offered our help to achieve a smooth transaction but were knocked back.

We went to a three-day Cash Machine workshop with Loral, as we knew she would teach us exactly what we needed.

We loved her message and after the workshop didn't hesitate to join her one-year Big Table program — even though it was a considerable expense when we were in a huge battle along with having over $300,000 of unsold stock on our hands. It was money well spent in the long run.

We are only seven months into our first year with Loral and the results speak for themselves. We have successfully re-launched our handmade jewellery range. We have also grown a second brand we import from overseas using new skills. We have learned to take a completely different approach to how we conduct our business. We carry out our due diligence, always get lawyers and accountants advice when in doubt, have expanded our skill base, and are open to learning.

We have enjoyed success and made mistakes, but most importantly we have learned from them. During 2009, we could have easily felt sorry for ourselves, closed down, and spent years licking our wounds. But this would not have been in our character. We came from nothing, built something special, and went back to the beginning.

▨ THE RISE ... AGAIN

TODAY WE ENJOY success once again. Maybe not to the same scale but we are much better off. We have set our priorities right and work toward building a great team around us who share our passion and goals. We have systems in place and are part of the Live Out Loud community, which is a wealth of information, knowledge, wisdom, and support.

▨ OUR TIMELESS MESSAGE FOR YOU

- Invest in your education, as it will provide the best return on investment.

- Don't be afraid to ask for help and admit you made mistakes. You will always learn from them.

- ♦ Always carry out due diligence when entering an agreement.

- ♦ Have an exit plan with all suppliers, in case things go wrong.

- ♦ When your child is talking to you about your business at the age of one, remember to leave work at work.

■ *Meet the Contributors*

MANUELA ROCKER IS the co-founder and director of Seriously Twisted Jewellery Pty Ltd. Born in Switzerland and having worked in the bank and insurance industry, she decided she needed to see the world. The most economical way to do this was to utilize her skills (fluency in four languages) and became a flight attendant for a Swiss business airline. In 1995 Manuela moved permanently to Australia. In 2003 she met Megan Wisheart who has been her friend and business partner ever since. Manuela lives in Manly Beach with her partner Carl and their four-year-old son Jett.

Contact Manuela at www.seriouslytwisted.com.au

MEGAN WISHEART WAS born in New Zealand and always had a flair for creativity. She was an award-winning creative in advertising for twenty years before discovering her passion to be her own boss. Her love of design and fashion moved her in a new direction after having her first child. An early childhood love of jewellery making steered her into the business she is in today. After meeting Manuela Rocker at the Manly Art and Crafts Market, they formed a relationship that grew into a successful jewellery business. Megan and her partner Jon live with their two children, Lewis and Niki on the northern beaches of Sydney.

Contact Megan at www.nikiandjett.com

Bringing Vision Into Reality

Darron Dickinson

My first effort at entrepreneurship happened at seventeen when I bought a mail-order car lock entry kit and started "The Lock Doctors." It was 1989, and answering machines still recorded on magnetic tape, while very few homes, if any, had call waiting. The only cell phone I remember being used in any practical sense was Gordon Gekko's Motorola DynaTac (known as "the brick") while he paced around giving Bud Fox directions about what to do with Blue Star.

The Lock Doctors business model was simple: charge people thirty-five dollars to travel on-site and unlock their car-doors. My fleet vehicle, which I owned due to income from the oldest Minnesota business model — neighborhood snow shoveler — was a slightly worn 1970 blue Oldsmobile Cutlass. The gas-gulper impressed my friends, but would have made any finance manager purse their lips while noting it in the expense column. So with a modest $150 initial investment for the lock kit, business cards, and a few dollars to market my venture, I set off to open doors.

From the beginning, there were a few factors inhibiting the success and expansion of The Lock Doctors:

1. I was still in high school, so business hours were limited to time slots not already filled with classes and football.

2. The answering machine and lifeline of the business was located at "the office," or as Mom often reminded me, the kitchen. We didn't have the fancier model that could be accessed remotely by a touchtone, so while in the field there was no practical way (other than calling home hoping someone was there) to check for new clients.

3. The office phone shared duties as the family's primary line and didn't have call waiting. I've often wondered how many potential customers huddled around the local gas station or grocery store payphone in minus fifteen-degree Minnesota temperatures, stringing together new and colorful versions of familiar adjectives.

Although a nice dose of nostalgia looking at a youthful endeavor containing plenty of learning experiences, The Lock Doctors never really had a chance.

Even though the details may differ, those who eventually found entrepreneurial success often have similar stories of an interest in business at a young age. And years later, after following many ideas, including a closet-full of different entrepreneurial hats, they mature into savvy decision makers and successful business owners.

Following high school, I took my parents' advice and went to college. On graduation, I spent the next eleven years in banking, working hard and performing well, which was often recognized, and I moved steadily up through the management ranks. I owe this progression in part to the following philosophy: Focus on your current duties, but perform at the next higher level so when the opportunity arises, which it always does, they already know that you can succeed in that role.

Instead of limiting myself to the straightforward tasks and responsibilities of my management position, I did extracurricular exercises, and tried to model my work in a consultant capacity. I practiced "what would I do if..." scenarios, and thought as though my employer had contracted me instead of simply employing me.

At thirty-four, I had risen to chief information officer of Collegiate Funding Services, a student-lending firm that was subsequently purchased by Chase Bank. When I launched my first consulting business,

I devised three ideas I thought were critical to success and eventual company sustainability:

- First, I called the most successful entrepreneurs I knew and asked them for wisdom. Their key piece of advice was to pick an industry and focus on it, especially since I, like most start-ups, had limited cash and resources.

- Second, I researched the top fifty Minnesota consulting firms that were led by the entrepreneurs. I sent each owner an introductory email asking if they would be willing to share their experience, and provide advice on building a successful firm. Those meetings became a valuable part of my networking program, and I maintain contact with several of them to this day. One interesting caveat, which speaks to the need to be creative when networking, is that I have received more job offers from pursuing that idea than I've had sending out traditional cover letters or resumes.

- Third, I engaged a business coach that held me accountable, provided insights, and asked the right questions that drew on my talents and skills.

Today, I am the founder and CEO of Glacierforce, LLC, a Growth Engineering firm that integrates and transforms systems and processes for companies in the financial services, mortgage, and student lending sectors nationwide. In its fourth year — through hard work, sacrifice, and occasional self-doubt — Glacierforce has grown from a start-up to a couple of million dollars in revenue per year.

I started the firm after being severed from Chase Bank. I had the opportunity to stay with Chase for a respectable salary and benefits, but chose (against the better judgment of family and friends) to forgo the safety of the corporate office and chase my entrepreneurial dreams.

GlacierForce did not start with its current name, but has adapted to the changing marketplace. It began in 2006 as Scholarmint, a consulting firm focused on student lending. Unfortunately, at the same time a legislative headwind had put the industry in turmoil. By mid-2007, the student lending industry was virtually eliminated by sweeping legislation. Some months later in an unfortunate double whammy, the current Great Recession began.

Fortunately, Scholarmint was a relatively new, financially modest company with few employees. We adapted quickly to the changing environment by broadening our focus to include all financial services. We changed the name to GlacierForce to deconstruct the connotation we only offered student-lending services.

During the first years, there were many times when the safety of a corporate position started to look pretty good, but we landed good contracts at key times that kept us afloat and gave us the ability to stay in and keep fighting for relevance. Our firm continues to grow, and we continue to work hard to provide clients with the best possible services.

An entrepreneur should have a company vision and a number to work for. I have the vision of building and owning a fifty-million-dollar company. My vision is for not one firm but an enterprise, and many times this has helped eliminate the tunnel vision that comes with thinking about short-term limitations, or when thinking gets too boxed in. A vision creates a landscape and palette to work with; even if you make a mistake here or there, a few misguided swipes of the brush won't mess up the whole canvas.

One of the keys to my success is to keep moving and try things when the first ideas do not succeed. Always be willing to say "yes" until you determine it does not fit with your desire or competence. Too often people take a perfectionist or wait-and-see approach. I've found by having confidence in yourself and not being afraid to dive in, you can get to work and start making things happen.

Back in high school I read an article about aging people and their regrets. In the study they found many of those interviewed did not regret the things they did, but the things they did not have the courage to do.

I often ask myself, in business as well as my personal life: Is this an opportunity I will regret if I don't try, or have regrets if I give up too early? To borrow a concept from Napoleon Hill in *Think and Grow Rich* — in which he discusses success as something that comes just past the point where that average person quits or stops three feet from gold — the challenge is determining if the current claim holds the riches, which is done through self analysis and expert opinion. Seek out those who have mined successfully ahead of you and ask for wisdom.

In retrospect, it would have been easy to quit and go back to a normal job, but the overwhelming desire to build a company that provides jobs, adds strength to the economy — while simultaneously providing a good income for my family — keeps me invigorated. There is an enormous sense of pride in building a business, and entrepreneurship provides a great opportunity to explore and challenge all your abilities.

I encourage fledgling entrepreneurs to nurture that deep yearning for independence, and to look at every challenge as an opportunity to learn, grow, reposition, and move forward. When you've started a new venture, be conservative on cash like it was your last dollar, and only hire the best people in your network that are capable of freeing you up to improve overall corporate performance. Be prepared to fire people quickly if they do not work out; they may end up costing precious resources or worse, the company itself.

Lastly, remember to have fun and find passion in your work, and the money will eventually find you.

▨ *Meet the Contributor*

DARRON DICKINSON HAS sixteen years' experience in financial services. He received a BA in economics/legal studies from Hamline University, an MBA in finance/strategic management from the Carlson School of Management, University of Minnesota, an MSCIS in information systems from the University of Phoenix, and a graduate certificate in entrepreneurship from the University of St. Thomas. His wonderful and supportive wife, Laura, has put up with his crazy ideas for eighteen years, with three beautiful children (Morgan is twelve, Dylan is ten, and Raegan is four). Contact Darron at www.glacierforce.com

THE EVOLUTION OF AN ENTREPRENEUR

Jayne Blumenthal (LBT #74)

FROM A YOUNG age I was a go-getter. My first lesson on the toils of being an entrepreneur came when I was in kindergarten, bursting with enthusiasm and happily bouncing my strawberry blonde pigtails. Using the back of my father's business cards, I generously invited my entire class to a party at my house for a Sunday afternoon. Of course, each of the nineteen children accepted my invitation. The problem was I neglected to tell my parents about the party until two hours before it started. Humiliated, I was forced to spend the better part of an hour calling each of my classmates to rescind my invitation. This was my first failure as a leader, but it taught me two of my greatest, and most unforgettable, lessons: always prepare, and understand the rules before starting.

As a young adult, I was hired out of fashion school as a clerk at a retail clothing firm and quickly advanced to garment buyer. My rapid progress was helped along by a solid work ethic, seemingly endless energy, and the desire to learn and overcome obstacles. These traits would help me when I ventured into the world of entrepreneurship. Working for others occupied the next ten years of my life, but at the age of twenty-nine, I changed courses. I married for the third time — and unlike my first two marriages, this time to a loving, supportive husband. My new husband already had a daughter and a son, and we immediately added to the family. With our first son only seventeen days old, we started a garment manufacturing business, and within a year we added twin boys to the brood.

By organizing my time, I split my efforts between caring for our demanding family and growing our new venture. I surrounded myself with the right kind of people that could help me achieve my goals, such as employees, nannies, contractors, and accountants, all of whom made it possible for me to focus on business. With our team, over the course of twenty years we turned the company into a multi-million dollar international enterprise.

Heading an international garment firm was comfortable for me. I enjoyed making deals and solving problems. But the most rewarding part of running our company wasn't the sales, the volume, or the money. It was connecting with the people. Early on, I learned that I had a knack for motivating our staff, for getting them to reach higher, work harder, and be more fulfilled in the process.

Fifteen years into the business, the way trade was conducted around the globe changed, and our current model was no longer viable. I believe a good businessperson knows how to adapt with her market, so when faced with these challenges, I hired a business coach to help me navigate the path. I was determined to find a way over, around, or straight through the obstacles we faced. The knowledge gained by working with my coach led to a shift in our methods and doubling of our sales. While that knowledge was valuable, through the process of being coached something completely unexpected occurred. I gained something even more valuable than doubling our sales: although I had great success in the garment industry, I discovered a completely new adventure. Given my inherent ability to understand and motivate people, it seemed a natural step to help others like myself. The vision for the rest of my professional life became clear. I wanted to help others overcome the obstacles that were stopping them from having the health, careers, and relationships they longed for. I knew there are many areas in which people could use help. Finding a niche would be essential, as it is in every business venture. It didn't take long to narrow it down. In fact, it was right in front of me all along.

Before I left the garment industry, I had a chronic infection that lasted over two years. I had neglected my health and justified it by saying there simply wasn't enough time. Consequently, I endured a long and difficult process that included multiple antibiotics, surgery, and a multitude of doctors. Ultimately, I took control of my health through study, holistic medicine, and old-fashioned determination. When I reflected on this time in my life, I realized there were women everywhere who were running families, managing companies, growing relationships, and ignoring their health as I had. Learning from my struggles, I reinvented myself as a Weight Loss Mentor and Coach for women to turn to.

The decision to leave our garment business was bold, and not without risk. Like any secure job, the safety net of a profitable business is hard to walk away from, but I trusted my skills enough to believe I could thrive. After closing down the company by wrapping up existing work, I began my new journey by completing the Hilton Johnson Health Coach Training Program. While I learned immensely from this curriculum, it somehow wasn't enough — my niche needed to be even more specific.

With the same eagerness I had as a schoolchild, I searched for the knowledge I knew would lead me to my unique forte. For six months I scoured the Internet, searching for others like myself so I could see what worked for them. I scanned countless pages of offerings for educational textbooks, webinars, courses, and systems. Blinded by enthusiasm and passion, I spent thousands of dollars on educational systems and seminars on every topic that was even remotely related to health and lifestyle coaching. While some of what I spent was well worth the investment, I was carried away by my childhood lesson of "always prepare." I learned the hard way it is possible to prepare too much, and I'm now much more thoughtful of my choices.

Throughout my educational adventures, what led me to my niche was the one thing that started me on my journey to begin with: connecting with people. My big breakthrough came when I decided to use Facebook to reach out to new "friends." Over a month's time, I added over seven hundred friends to my network. In itself, that is a useless accomplishment. What makes this special is that I spent hours each day reaching out to people, introducing myself, and cultivating real friendships. One of these friendships was with a woman who used a method called Emotional Freedom Techniques (EFT) to lose weight after years of fad and yo-yo dieting. When I looked into EFT and tried it on myself, I saw I was making strides where before I was making baby steps. That's when I knew I had found my special something.

EFT is the use of your fingertips to tap on specific acupressure points on the body, cleansing and rejuvenating the body's energy fields. This creates freedom from chronic problems and blockages that give roots to emotional and physical pain. EFT is known to help common problems such as weight loss, anxiety, depression, and performance issues — just to scratch the surface. The first client I used EFT on reported an immediate relief from her fear of abandonment plus a very practical side effect: relief from years of insomnia. All of the information on health and wellness I gathered during my search for knowledge became more valuable and amplified when I combined it with EFT. It is a quick, inexpensive way to get people moving in a new direction, and it perfectly suits my goal: to help as many people as possible, as quickly as possible.

By adding EFT expertise to my practice, I help my clients use what they've learned from their work with me, so they can make breakthroughs more quickly than ever before. I serve as their experienced teacher, who can impart knowledge of health, business, and relationship tactics that work. As their trusted advisor, I show them practical, customized actions for using their newfound knowledge. And as their effective motivator, I inspire them to keep moving in the direction of optimal health, no matter what is happening in their lives.

Keeping my entrepreneurial spirit high has presented its challenges throughout the years. There are always lessons to learn and obstacles to overcome. The one thing that keeps me moving is my belief that life is easier than it looks. Whatever happens to me, from illness, to divorce, to tragic losses, I insist on seeing the beauty and opportunity hidden along the way. It's this type of outlook that led me to success and my life's work — helping others to take control of their weight by teaching them to see that life truly is easier than it seems.

I am finally living my dream of helping people to break through self-imposed obstacles and change their lives. I watch my clients enjoy lives filled with vibrant health and lasting happiness, and that gives me more than enough motivation to keep on growing, imagining, and believing.

▣ Meet the Contributor

JAYNE BLUMENTHAL is a Weight Loss Mentor and Coach who uses EFT Tapping to teach people to take control of their weight in only 10 days without using extreme diets, dangerous pills, or insane exercise plans. Jayne's exceptional insight, understanding, and practical strategies lead her clients to quickly make dramatic changes that last. Jayne Blumenthal is a graduate of the Fashion Merchandising Institute, Canada, the Hilton Johnson Health Coach Training Program, the EFT Universe Level One program, and an alumnus of Loral's Big Table.

Contact Jayne at www.jayneblumenthal.com.

The Power of Belief

Michelle Prince (LBT #69)

THREE YEARS AGO I had a dream to become a best-selling author, inspirational speaker, and make a difference in the lives of people all over the world. The problem was it was just a dream. I had no idea how to make it happen.

In July 2008, a good friend of mine came to Dallas to attend a personal development seminar. My friend had created a goals program that she sold at these seminars. Since my background had always been in sales, and she was a lifelong friend, I offered to help sell her products for three days while she attended the conference. I had no way of knowing this decision would completely change my life.

At this time, I worked a corporate job and lived an ordinary life. I had greater aspirations for myself but couldn't get past my fears. Every time I allowed myself to dream about my future, my fears and self doubt seeped in to convince me not only was it not possible, but that I wasn't capable. I remained in this holding pattern for twelve years.

I wish I knew then how to let go of my fears and just go for it. After all, I had worked for the master of motivation, Zig Ziglar, early in my career. I learned from Zig how to set goals and overcome obstacles, but somewhere along the way I forgot what I learned and gave into the temptation of thinking happiness and success were for others and not me.

Why is it so many of us as adults give up on our dreams? Why was it so much easier to dream when we were kids? I'm sure you daydreamed of what you wanted to be when you were growing up. Back then opportunities seemed endless and our dreams were all within our reach. However, somewhere along the way many of us lost track of those dreams and the belief we could do anything worthwhile.

Somewhere deep inside, there is still that kid who knows what you really want out of life. It could be writing a book, starting a business, or taking that trip. The problem is, we push those dreams to the back of our minds and minimize their importance because they seem too big or too bold. Before long, we forget about them all together.

But if you just take the time to look within yourself and discover that passion again, you can dust off those dreams and put together a plan to go after them. It's only then that life starts to get really exciting. Trust me, I should know.

I knew I loved personal development but I couldn't get my arms around how I could make a living in that area. After all, I wasn't a speaker or an author. I felt like I had nothing to offer in this area so I continued down the path of just working for a living instead of living to work.

At one point, I got honest and thought about what I really wanted to be, do, and have. I kept coming back to speaking and seminars and having an impact on people's lives like Zig Ziglar had for many years. I wouldn't dare admit, but my real goal was to be like Zig. I'd catch myself and unconsciously think, "Who do you think you are? How dare you think you could ever be like Zig Ziglar? Get over yourself and get back to your normal life." And so I did, until the day I decided to help my friend at her seminar.

I've always been inspired at seminars and being surrounded by like-minded individuals who share my passion for personal development. That's not typical of most people, and certainly not my neighbors, family, or some of the friends who were surrounding me at that time. For me, I light up when I'm at a seminar or around other people who are trying to better themselves — people who are motivated and want more for their life, and have goals. I get fired up, and that's exactly what happened to me at this event.

I'm not sure if it was the timing of the seminar or a word spoken by one of the speakers, but something shifted in me that day. It was as if someone hit me over the head and I had that "a-ha" moment. For many years, I'd been saying, "Not me. Who am I to do this?"

But on this day, I said to myself, "Why not me? I have a unique story to tell. I've gone through some situations that people can relate to. I'm not perfect, but I've learned so many things through the years on how to improve myself and I want to share this."

It occurred to me that if I had issues with self-esteem and goal setting after working for Zig Ziglar all those years, others might be struggling, too. Maybe there were people who never heard of goal setting and didn't know where to start. I could help them. That's what prompted me to go and do just that. A light bulb went off and I have never looked back.

In order to create a happy life you must believe in yourself. Believe you can do something before you can set out to do it. If you don't have the belief in yourself, you won't be able to accomplish anything.

We're all unique, we all have special gifts, we all have a purpose, and it's our job to find that purpose and then live our lives fulfilling it. But so many are held back by self-limiting beliefs, just like I was. They don't believe they can accomplish their goals, so subconsciously they sabotage their chance of success or don't bother trying.

You have to believe in yourself in order for others to believe in you. People treat you with the same amount of respect as you treat yourself. If you don't have the confidence you can do a good job, no one else is going to believe you can. It all starts with you.

It took a long time, but I finally made a decision that day to follow my heart and to go after my goal. I went home from the seminar and began to write. Having never written before, I figured I'd have trouble but the words flew out of me. I had the entire book written in three weeks. For someone who thought they had nothing to say, I was amazed to see how much had been in me waiting to come out.

Fast forward a few years and I'm humbled and proud to say I am a best-selling author, sought after motivational speaker, life mentor, radio host, certified Zig Ziglar motivational speaker, and happier than I've ever been. And all of this was done while I was working a full time job. It started with a decision, with me taking a leap of faith and believing in myself.

I'm no different from you. I'm a wife, mother, daughter, and sister, just trying to do my best day in and day out like everyone else. But I am passionate about life, and about achieving my goals. I've had that passion for a long time and I followed my dreams, which is why I'm sharing my story with you.

What about you? What do you really want out of life? What dream do you have that you don't dare tell anyone or believe you can accomplish? If I can do it, so can you. Don't waste another moment delaying your dreams. Your life is short and you are given one chance to make it the best, so why not go for it? If you believe you can, I know you will be able to accomplish big goals. I believe in you, and so does that kid deep inside.

Meet the Contributor

MICHELLE PRINCE IS the author of the best-selling book, *Winning in Life Now … How to Break Through to a Happier You!* She has been endorsed by and worked for some of the most influential, successful motivational teachers and authors in the industry, including Zig Ziglar.

Michelle has embraced personal development, goal setting, and the desire to improve her life since the age of eighteen. She has taken that knowledge to transform not only her own life, but the lives of millions of people who want to break through to a life of greatness.

Aside from being an author, Michelle is a sought after motivational speaker, one-on-one mentor, and radio show host on the "Winning In Life Now" radio show. She owns her own company, Prince Performance Group, as well as her own publishing company, Performance Publishing. Michelle is a certified Zig Ziglar motivational speaker and shares her talent across the country representing the Ziglar organization. She has hosted "Ziglar's Success 2.0 LIVE" webcasts and has been featured on SIRIUS Satellite Radio as well as several syndicated radio shows across the country. Contact Michelle at www.winninginlifenow.com

If I Can Succeed, You Can Too

Sandra L. Wales (LBT #76)

THE WORLD OF entrepreneurs and role models for their development was not the world I was raised in. My father worked for Shell Oil from age seventeen through to his retirement at age fifty-three. He had a job that provided a secure and comfortable life for his family, and he was rewarded with a good pension and the support of his company for his loyalty. As a child, I asked my father at the supper table, "What did you do at work today, Dad?"

"The same as yesterday," he replied. His response never varied. I always wanted to understand what adults did with their lives. His answer seemed so unfulfilling, and I was puzzled.

I was destined to not fit the mould of the secure daily job. I obtained a degree in music, followed my interest in spirituality, and then started in the corporate finance world. I worked in large and small corporations, thinking this would be the source of a secure future for myself. I followed the right steps by obtaining an MBA from a private university and getting promoted up the corporate ladder to Chief Financial Officer. I always believed I could attain much more for the companies I was with. Politics and the lack of a culture that wanted to move ahead and provide a good product in the company seemed to hold me back. I wanted to make a difference in people's lives and help them. In 2001 after having to layoff a number of employees, I could not sign up for another twenty years of the daily grind without helping humanity. The work focus was pointless and I could not make a difference in the world.

In 2003 I became the reluctant entrepreneur. I was frightened with my decision to found my own company and move outside of my comfort zone. I had tried to avoid being an entrepreneur but against my better judgment I forged ahead. I looked at my skill set, which was running companies and a diversified financial background. Then I asked myself how I could use my work of the past twenty years to help people.

This led me to found Wales Investments, Inc., a wealth management company that offers money management, comprehensive financial planning, real estate investing, tax preparation for individuals and corporations, and corporate pension design. I polished my credentials in this area and added to my existing accounting license by obtaining a CFP® (Certified Financial Planner) certificate and a real estate license. I took a position at UCSC to teach pension design and retirement planning, and further develop my experience and give back.

I learned about money from my father, who had very good financial planning instincts. He paid our house off when he was thirty-nine years old, never had any debt, took us on five-week vacations every year, and successfully planned his retirement (with the help of Shell). I remember at age six going to the local bank where my father had me open up my own bank account; this got me excited about putting money in my account throughout the years. The learning stayed with me throughout my life. I paid for my own university education and graduated with no loans and a grant to study in London, England at Trinity College. I received my MBA from a private university paid for by the technology company where I worked.

This upbringing supported me in the development of my business. I decided not to borrow money or outlay too much at the beginning. I kept costs down by working out of my home for three years, and eventually purchased my own office condo. Many new entrepreneurs go into large amounts of debt at the start up, which puts much more risk on the operation. The role of the entrepreneur is that of a long distance runner, not a sprinter. You need to conserve your energy, and money is a type of energy.

The old adage is, if you don't track it, you don't know whether what you are doing is what you really want. Business owners will start up and never think to hire a bookkeeper to track the results of their endeavors. It is important to purchase Quickbooks and start the tracking from the beginning.

For example, you need to know what you spent your energy (money) on and create quarterly profit and loss reports and balance sheets. Set yourself financial goals and measure them. You can look at what you achieved and measure your net worth annually. This is one measure of your overall success you need to pay attention to. If you are not tracking your business goals you don't have a business — you have a hobby.

Employees are one of the most important and valuable resources in any business. If you create your business online and outsource your processes, you can create a greater profit to the bottom line. If you are in a service business like mine, that is not possible. Hire carefully and slowly so you create the culture and profit margins that will build wealth for you. I have worked for Fortune 500 companies and some of the greatest mistakes I see are over hiring, especially in the management area, and not putting enough technology to manage the processes. The large companies have no loyalty toward their employees and treat their employment line like a revolving door. What they do not understand is that every time a seasoned employee leaves, years of knowledge go with them that will take years to replicate. Your leadership and development of your employees is key to the creative growth of your company. Some of the worst mistakes I made was hiring employees that cost the company and brought no value. If you make this mistake, terminate the employee as soon as you can. It will not get any better.

Take the time to develop your employees and develop yourself. Educate yourself emotionally and spiritually, and strive to be the best in your industry. Meet your employees and ask them for their suggestions on how to improve your processes, serve your clients, and grow your business. A culture of respect for employees and clients goes a long way to growing your business.

The next important point is that you cannot give leadership to your company if you do not know yourself. Know your strengths and your weaknesses, what you like to do versus what you do not like to do. Your responsibility is to inspire your culture and employees to create the best product or service for your customers. One thing I have observed in Fortune 500 companies is that the culture of the CEO is the culture of the company. This is true of companies with 160,000 employees or five employees.

Another lesson I have learned over the years is to have multiple streams of income. For example, in my business, the tax return area is steady and recurring; consulting provides a monthly income; and comprehensive financial planning provides income on a project basis while money management produces yet another source of revenue. Look at your business and think of the different income streams you can produce, and then analyze these on a quarterly basis to understand the characteristics of each revenue stream and how the different macroeconomic environments affect your income streams. Just as asset allocation and diversification reduces the overall risk of your portfolio, different streams of revenue reduces the risk of the development of your company.

The satisfaction of working with individuals and corporations to create the retirement and life they have dreamed about is compelling. I appreciate using my financial knowledge to improve people's wealth and financial stability.

Starting my company has been the most exhilarating and personal growth education. I was concerned about starting the company since I was raised in a secure employment oriented family. Know yourself and ask whether you are comfortable in a corporate environment or always seem to envision a better way of running a company and want to make improvements that the current corporate culture won't allow. If the latter scenario describes you, take the leap and know that the new entrepreneurial environment will welcome and support you. It may be more damaging to your personal development to swallow the corporate mismatch and keep soldiering on. Speak with business owners in your industry and complete your due diligence about the company you want to start. Know yourself, and if your passion is to build a company, then do your homework and start your business. You could be the next reluctant entrepreneur, and remember, if I can create a successful company, so can you.

Meet the Contributor

SANDRA L. WALES, MBA, CMA, CFP® is the president of Wales Investments Inc. a wealth manager with twenty-seven years of experience in the financial sector. She currently teaches retirement planning and pension design at UCSC. Sandra has over twenty-two years' experience as a business and finance executive with Fortune 500 companies such as Silicon Graphics and Gap Inc., as well as venture capital. From her background in business finance, including experience with high-ranking executives and business owners in the domestic and international arenas, Sandra has gained a highly valuable skill set. She works on strategic as well as operational aspects of businesses, allowing her to aid business owners with retirement planning and to help individuals grow their wealth and plan for the financial independence they have always dreamed of. Contact Sandra at www.walesinvestments.com

From Ordinary to Extraordinary

John Limbocker (LBT #69)

My entrepreneurial career started as a preteen. "Anything for a buck" was my motto. I realized people needed things and were willing to pay for them. I made money with everything from washing cars to building cabinets.

Our neighbor had a business making computerized ignition systems to increase gas mileage for cars. This was revolutionary at the time and they were selling like hotcakes. I visited his shop and saw a huge pile of the systems in his trash bin. He explained many people didn't know how to install the devices and would short them out and return them. I asked if I could take a few home to play with.

My father, being an electrical engineer, helped me build a piece of test equipment and we found that over fifty percent of the systems were operational. I went back to my neighbor and offered to test every one and repackage those that worked for resale for five dollars each and he agreed.

My first business was born. I made about twenty bucks an hour, which was very impressive. After a couple months I recommended that a diode be placed in the circuit to prevent the units from shorting out when hooked up backwards. If the customer hooked the system up backwards all they had to do was switch the two wires and it would work without damaging the unit.

This great idea unfortunately put me out of business. At the young age of thirteen my first lesson in business was learned: "You need to be valuable but not replaceable."

At the age of fifteen I worked with my brother making fiberglass parts for model airplanes. This grew into a sizable manufacturing business. He was the salesman and I was the workforce. I developed assembly line procedures to put out massive amounts of product with minimal labor.

At sixteen all my friends had jobs in fast food and even though I made fifty times what they did, they were having fun while I was alone in a warehouse cranking out fiberglass products. So I wanted to join and applied at the same places they did so we could work together. To my surprise, McDonald's wouldn't even hire me. Imagine not having any control over your destiny and being dependent on someone for a job. I said to hell with that. That's when I decided I would never put myself in a position of depending on anyone. My success was up to me and no one else.

After years of getting my hands dirty while working with my brother in fiberglass, it was time to clean up my act and work for myself. On my twenty-first birthday I opened my current business, Limbo Vision, Inc. With a last name of Limbocker, I was always referred to as Limbo and this was going to be my vision so I felt it was an appropriate name.

It started off as commercial product photography and special effects. I always had a knack for solving problems and being able to do what others could not. This fused with me as my first belief in business, which was to be invaluable and not replaceable. I always look at things as, "If anyone can do it, so what?" I never wanted to be a "so what."

My business grew very quickly but it was years later before I recognized why. I had always been a master at my craft, whatever it was at the time. So many people knew this about me that referrals came out of nowhere. I shared what I was doing with my clients and they referred people that needed my help.

When I changed what I was doing, my customers followed me and continued buying completely different services from me and kept referring their peers. The digital era came around in the mid-nineties and my profession became obsolete. Being quick-minded, I saw the opportunity of providing website services to my existing customers and it was an immediate success. All my clients needed it and were happy to pass that business to me.

It wasn't until recently I realized all of the business I had was from prospects referred by a trusted source and pre-sold prior to contacting me. This became obvious a few years ago when I decided to expand. I made the decision to proactively market my business rather than just take what came along, which was always more than good enough. It was quite an eye opener when I started going after prospects that didn't know me. The big shocker was I had no sales skills. I realized then I had always depended on others for that.

About the same time, the movie *The Secret* came out and explained why I had always been successful. I always put out that I could do anything and that was mirrored back to me. But the movie also opened my eyes to the fact there was a lot I could learn from others and the importance of mentorship. I began traveling to events and listening to speakers related to sales and business strategy.

I learned that sales are the foundation to any real business. You can have a booming business with a less than mediocre product if you know how to sell it. At the same time you, can have the best product or service on the planet but your business will fail if you can't sell it.

This was backed by the fact that so many people in my industry, which is now Search Engine Optimization (SEO), didn't have a clue as to what they were doing yet they had multi-million dollar businesses that were growing like wildfire. I knew if I had a sales process I could grow my business as big as I wanted.

I started my first mentorship with Eric Lofholm who taught me sales are a learned skill. Eric said, "The shortest path to success is to follow the footsteps of those who have already achieved it. Success leaves footprints. Follow the tracks and you will find it."

Eric opened my eyes to the fact I was selling the wrong thing. I was trying to sell SEO and he told me no one wants SEO. He said, "Your prospects want leads, new customers, and more business and that is what you provide. Offer them what they want and they will buy it."

Another valuable thing I learned from Eric was to identify people of influence who have a relationship with your ideal clients and have them endorse you and refer you to their peers. With very little effort I identified a few key people of influence and started building those relationships.

I found most of the people of influence for my target audience were also mentors like Loral Langemeier, John Assaraf, Perry Belcher, and Ryan Deiss. My plan was to learn from them, and then enter into their communities and contribute back. Many of the things I learned and relationships that have formed from my participation in these communities have been worth one hundred times the cost. I no longer consider mentorship an expense — it has proven to be the most lucrative investment imaginable.

I learned the only limits I had were ones I created for myself. By reprogramming my internal belief system (or inner game, as John Assaraf refers to it) I am now able to get anything I ever wanted. My business has taken off to levels I never thought possible.

Today my main business is getting business owners in front of their ideal clients as they search online for the products and services the business owner offers. I have put together an online training program for those business owners that want to do it themselves or have their in-house team do it. This program greatly reduces or even eliminates the learning curve and helps my clients avoid costly mistakes. I offer several free webinars as well as interviews explaining some of the best ways to leverage the Internet and grow your business cost-effectively. The game has changed as far as how businesses are getting new customers and I am solving it, one happy business owner at a time.

▨ Meet the Contributor

JOHN LIMBOCKER is founder and CEO of Internet Dominators, servicing hundreds of businesses. He is a master SEO strategist, specializing in getting his clients to the top of the organic listings on the major search engines using their most lucrative keywords.

John is a sought-after speaker at major events like the Web 2.0 Conference, Ryan Deiss's Traffic Conversion Conference, and Stompernet. He also freely shares his knowledge in interviews and recently developed an online training program to teach webmasters and website owners all of his tricks in his new SEO Dominator's Club.

John lives and works inside a tropical estuary at Huntington Beach, California he created and calls LimboLand.

Contact John at www.internetdominators.com

From Concept to Cash

Creating Multiple Streams of Niche Market Revenue

John C. Robinson (LBT #10)

▪ Finding Your Passion, With a Twist

Whatever I do to earn a living must meet one basic criterion: it has to be fun. This was the challenge I gave myself when I was just seventeen years old. That challenge has served me well and allowed me to live and work on my passion for over thirty years.

Earning a degree in biology resulted from my love for nature, birds, and the outdoors. Likewise, publishing my first book in 1990 was a natural extension of my love for writing, which I had practiced for fifteen years at that time. The topic of my book? You guessed it — birds.

Many people claim they're searching for their passion. I chuckle when I hear this, because your passion finds you. Regardless of how you come to identify your passion, you might ask, "How can I turn my passionate interest in this topic into a successful entrepreneurial venture?"

Sadly, most people never take the next step. Of those that do, many give up out of frustration with limited results. In this chapter, I've laid out the blueprint for how anyone can create a sustainable income in a niche market by using their passion to enrich the lives of others.

■ PROOF OF CONCEPT

YOUR BUSINESS SHOULD uniquely leverage your skills and expertise to benefit others. However, to create real success, you need full understanding of the entrepreneurial landscape specific to your niche. Who are your competitors? What do they offer? How can you add value in your niche and distinguish yourself in the process?

The answers to these questions arise from interviewing your competitors and/or becoming a customer or partner (yes, you can partner with your competitors).

In 1999, I decided to combine my passion for bird watching with my skills and expertise in writing and database design to design a business around a software product for bird enthusiasts. I purchased all the products in my competitive space, studied them, and identified a more streamlined approach, providing more benefits to the consumer than had previously been offered in a single application. The result was that my product was carried in retail outlets such as Best Buy and CostCo for several years, with as many as 8,000 units being ordered at one time.

Interestingly, years later Loral Langemeier introduced me to this process of becoming your competition's customer and evaluating the entrepreneurial landscape as the concept behind the "Model Company."

■ DO YOU KNOW YOUR TARGET AUDIENCE?

IN ADDITION TO studying competitors, you must also study your consumer. Before I developed my software product, I scrutinized numerous product reviews and surveyed likely prospects. I identified a short list of benefits and features that needed to be included in my software for it to be successful. For example, people in my target market want to learn how to identify birds without experiencing the frustration that often accompanies the process. By building an intuitive software application that facilitates bird identification and doubles as an educational resource for children, I was able to offer a tool that was popular with parents, teachers, and students alike.

However, success comes in stages. Despite the appeal of my software application, there were also many complaints. Regardless of how much the complaints may hurt your ego, this is not the time to give up. I continued to survey my customers to identify how to make the application more user-friendly. Of even greater value were the surveys I gave to my prospects that opted not to buy my product. What features and benefits could I add to influence them to purchase?

By the time version 5.0 of the software was released, my user surveys paid off. At tradeshows, it was not uncommon for people to purchase before I asked for the sale.

Surveying the customers and prospects in your target market is required for success in any business. Large companies resort to full-scale consumer segmentation studies that allow them to distinguish different consumer groups in their target market and identify the groups that will deliver the greatest return on investment for their marketing dollar.

ESTABLISH YOURSELF AS AN EXPERT

IF YOUR BUSINESS represents something you have studied for many years, you are likely an expert on the product or service you offer. That's why I always say "We are the undiscovered heroes in our own business." You can establish yourself as an expert by creating a flagship information product that solves a critical need for the consumers in your target market.

An information product can be a book, workbook, audio CD, DVD, or a recorded teleseminar or webinar class. Many entrepreneurs imagine themselves writing a book. If you choose this path, your book can be published through traditional means, self-published, or a work-for-hire under contract. My biggest mistake when I began publishing was thinking it was best to use traditional means of publishing. I later learned self-publishing offered distinct advantages, including speed to market, more control over the entire process, and a greater share of the profit potential.

By establishing yourself as an expert in your market, you give yourself credibility and a reason for the prospect to believe your products or services will meet their needs.

■ REPURPOSE THE CONTENT OF YOUR INFORMATION PRODUCT

YOU CAN REPURPOSE the content in your information product into a variety of other products or services to create additional revenue streams for your business. Your goal is to create a sales funnel that allows your prospects to choose the product or service that meets their needs at any point in time.

For example, as a business coach for entrepreneurial authors, the content I teach in my six-week webinar on information product development has been repurposed into a free report, a booklet sold for one dollar, a thirty dollar per month membership site, a one hundred dollar strategy call, and a multi-thousand dollar year-long coaching program. The hidden gem of repurposed content is paid public speaking, a practice I employ in my businesses two to three times each month. I frequently speak about goal setting and goal achieving, yet the majority of my speech uses examples and stories of the success I created by writing and selling books about birds, nature, and the outdoors.

Design your product or service to solve a clearly identified need in your consumer market. Products that make you happy or only serve to highlight the depth of your knowledge surrounding your subject matter often don't resonate well with consumers. Are you beginning to see the value of conducting objective customer and prospect surveys?

■ DESIGN AND IMPLEMENT A MARKETING AND SALES PLAN

WHEN I MET Loral, she saw the entrepreneurial potential I possessed. One of her first recommendations was to get a team to support me. I fought her on this one because the amount of income my business generated would not cover the expense of bringing a team on board. Months went by, then a year.

Nearly eighteen months after Loral gave me that advice, a $20,000 business opportunity was presented to me. The choice was clear: either I created a team to handle the additional breadth of responsibilities or kept the status quo. I got the team.

Today I have web designers, copywriters, financial analysts, a CPA, attorneys, and virtual assistants who work in or on my business. I once conducted an evaluation of my income before and after forming my team. The result was astonishing: my business' income had tripled following the hiring of the team members.

If you find yourself doing all the product development, web development, administrative support, accounting and bookkeeping, marketing, and sales for your business, you need a team. It is most relevant to talk about team in connection with where it can help or hurt your business the most: the net profit. You increase your net profit with effective marketing and sales. Let me ask the question again: do you have a team and the confidence to lead it?

Grow your marketing and sales team by hiring results-driven marketing services under contract while you handle sales and close the leads yourself. As your income grows, bring in a salesperson that closes the leads in exchange for commission or commission plus salary compensation. Affiliate partners also represent another easy way for most entrepreneurs to expand their sales force.

If you've chosen well, your team will create a high quality marketing and sales plan for your business. It's up to you to lead this process versus doing it yourself. Your willingness to get out of your own way and relinquish the hold on your incoming revenue streams starts today.

▨ GIVING BACK

THE ONE REGRET I have as an entrepreneur was not creating the plan to "give back" sooner than I did. Giving back encompasses work with a non-profit that benefits a noteworthy cause in alignment with your core beliefs and values.

As a biologist and student of nature, I believe it is important to have as many people as possible (especially our children) develop an interest in nature and the outdoors. As our nation becomes more culturally diverse with each passing decade, this need becomes even more urgent. Can you imagine a time when national parks like Yosemite and Yellowstone no longer grace our landscape?

I was the undiscovered hero in my own business. As an African American bird watcher, I noticed very few people like me actively study birds and visit national parks or refuges. I decided to write a book investigating this disparity and identifying solutions to help introduce nature and the outdoors to inner city and minority youth and young adults. Today I travel across continents to speak about my book.

I have since created a non-profit entity, the International Institute for Bird Watching. Its intent is to donate a percentage of the sales of my products and services to benefit underserved youth by introducing them to nature and a healthier way of life.

I encourage all of you to think of how you can give back to an important cause of your own. Entrepreneurial success is about bringing added value to the lives of others. Think about whom you could help today. You'll be glad you did.

■ Meet the Contributor

JOHN C. ROBINSON is an award-winning author and an in-demand speaker who has shared the stage with the top business development speakers and financial strategists of our generation. In 1979, John found his passion for the world of birds, nature, and the outdoors. Since then, he has written and published six books, led clients on natural history tours around the world, and authored the computer program code for nature-based software which has sold hundreds of thousands of copies (www.onmymountain.com). Contact John at www.earnprofitsfromyourpassion.com

PROFIT FROM YOUR SOCIAL MEDIA MARKETING BY "NETWORKING"

Katrina Sawa (LBT #76)

MY JOURNEY AS an entrepreneur started back in 2002. I'd held three corporate sales and marketing jobs over the five and a half years since college but the last one was the worst.

I was tired of inconsistent and inauthentic managers or bosses who thought they knew it all yet had no idea how to take care of their customers or motivate their employees. Off to the world of entrepreneurship I went. I wasn't scared, which was interesting to me considering how many entrepreneurs I talk to every month and the high percentage of them who were scared or hesitant to go out on their own.

Many entrepreneurs I've noticed have fears around:

* The unknown

* If they will be successful

* If anyone will buy from them

* And many other worries that go through their minds at the time

I didn't have those back then and I now know why that was. I had complete confidence in myself, and complete faith that whatever I did would work out. Don't ask me how, I just did.

This is one of the main things that make me an inspiring and motivating business coach. When I started my business, I began as a marketing consultant. I would network and focus on my local town and surrounding areas. I had previous clients from my other jobs that were the perfect target prospects for my new services so it made sense to start by calling on them. I built up the confidence to charge for my time and expertise. One by one, my customers purchased my services instead of buying ads in the local newspaper — the business that I was in before, selling advertising. They thought I had good ideas and strategies, but I didn't charge enough when I started. I had the "I'm new" mentality, which caused me to have uncertainty around my worth.

Over time that changed and I inched myself up to almost $200 per hour; it became easier to charge more once my clients were happy with my work and advice. I built my business on networking and follow up; that's pretty much all I did for about three years. I got good at it, too. Many business owners hate to network and have no idea how to follow up effectively so in that regard I was blessed. Networking is a learned trait, though; if this is you, you can get better at it if you learn proven skills and systems, and if you practice.

I went to fourteen or more networking events every month consistently for three years. I set up systems for follow-up including what to email or mail to everyone I met. I called almost everyone I met, too. It was a flawless plan and it built me a high five-figure business, replacing my job income. I still did it all myself, however.

I didn't have a clear plan on what I was doing or where I would take my business. All I knew was to network, follow up, and treat my clients well. I could never have planned for what my business looks like now.

Something was missing, though. How could I get to the six-figure mark without working more hours than there were in the day? Then it came to me. Global Internet marketing was missing.

Until you open yourself up to learn new things and also to new ideas or mentors, you never know what you don't know. I learned more than I ever thought I would know about leveraged revenue streams, effective Internet marketing, websites, targeting my business globally rather than just locally, and also how to systematize it and delegate so I could do more and reach more people without working much harder.

Over the next couple years I transformed my business. I started new group programs, memberships, live events, and teleclasses. Essentially, I developed products that allowed me to sell my expertise online. It began a whole new platform for my business. With the changes, I decreased the amount of time I was working with clients from sixty hours a week to ten. However, my income wasn't inching up that fast.

I wanted to know what else I could do to push me over that six-figure mark. I hired mentors and coaches and it wasn't until I hired a business coach that works more on mindset that I finally figured out what my block was. It was love. I had a good level of confidence but I didn't love myself nor did I have love in my life, which I desperately wanted at the time.

I learned over the course of that year it isn't always about the doing; many times it's about who we are that makes us more successful, more money, and gives us more love. That year I didn't develop or launch anything new in my business. Instead, I focused on me, my love life, and doing the basics to keep the business going. That's the year I hit six-figures.

Overcoming beliefs about myself was something that changed my life forever. I became even more confident as well as a more spiritually guided and inspiring business and marketing coach.

■ AFTER YOU HIT SIX FIGURES YOU WANT SEVEN

FOUR YEARS AGO I started networking more online on sites such as MySpace and LinkedIn. I posted profiles all over the Internet on whichever sites seemed to get a lot of traffic by small business owners and women entrepreneurs, who were my primary target market.

I knew this social media stuff would be important so I was trying to learn whatever I could to maximize my exposure on these sites. These days I mainly focus on sites like Facebook and LinkedIn and a few focused forums and membership sites, however I have a presence on almost every site that I've seen along the way too.

I still couldn't plan then for what happened since. My business plans now are in the form of vision boards with my top seven to eight goals for the year and pictures of what I want. I've learned this planning strategy works better for me.

Every year I envision what it is I want my life to look like or what else I want to add to my life and business. I crunch some numbers and plot basic strategies, but nothing too formal. That strategy doesn't work for everyone but it is an option if you're more of a big picture, big vision oriented and creative thinker.

Within a year of networking on social media sites, I had profiles and actively participated on more than twenty-five different sites. I soon developed a style of how to approach new people, on Facebook especially. I used the basic networking strategies I normally used at in-person events, except online. Whatever I was doing was working and brought me new coaching clients.

About a year ago I turned what I was doing into a now-proven system of how to interact personally while reaching thousands on Facebook and other social sites. I even delegated part of it, the initial, time-consuming part. In 2010 on average, a third of my new clients every month came from Facebook and specifically my "Profit From Social Media Marketing System." Now I teach it to my clients and sell it on my website for others to implement into their businesses.

If you haven't embraced the social media marketing craze yet or think it's going to go away, think again. You can be successful regardless of your business or industry with an interactive system for your social media, email and other marketing activities, multiple business processes, team building, and more.

If you're a little intimidated with the online world, think about it as a big networking event; if you're intimidated by networking, learn the strategies and tips that can help you feel more comfortable and confident. After all, it's the least expensive, most effective form of marketing you can do.

You can take your business to the next level using low-cost business and marketing basics like networking and follow-up, both online and offline. Systematize and automate or delegate much of what needs to be done on a monthly basis in your business in order to reach a larger number of prospects. When you do this, you'll see greater success.

▨ Meet the Contributor

KATRINA SAWA is known as the JumpStart Your Biz coach because she kicks her clients and their businesses into high gear online and fast. Katrina is the creator of the JumpStart Your Marketing® system and author of the book, *Love Yourself Successful*. She specializes in helping entrepreneurs start, grow, and market a business they're passionate about and ultimately take them to six-figure plus in revenue. Katrina has been featured in many print and online publications, television news shows, and on the *Oprah and Friends* XMRadioNetwork. She hosts her own radio show "JumpStart Your Business NOW" on Blog Talk Radio and speaks at business conferences all over the US. Contact Katrina or pick up her free gifts at www. jumpstartyourmarketing.com

The Journey to Your Passion

How Challenges Can Be Gifts

Dawn Stebbing (LBT #76)

I am a fashion beauty expert. I teach women and men how to save time and money by creating a stress-free wardrobe where they look fabulous every time they walk out their door.

I wasn't always into fashion but I always admired beautiful women. When I was little, I would say to myself, "Someday I want to look just like her." I believe when you say things to yourself out loud, you internalize it and own it and I did just that.

That took me to where I am today, but it wasn't an easy task. I grew up in a large, strict Catholic family where I was not encouraged to go on to college. I knew I never wanted to settle — there was something bigger and better for me out there and it was up to me to find it. I had a lot of challenges along the way.

With six other siblings and me being the second to the oldest girl, I learned very fast how to feed babies, change diapers, and clean house. I was responsible for taking care of my brothers and sisters as both parents had full time jobs outside the home.

Growing up in a big family presented many challenges for me, including:

1. The expectation level for achievement was very high.

2. I didn't get the attention I deserved.

3. When I did anything wrong I was punished severely for it — not what I called fun.

I started work at the age of seven. Nowadays you wouldn't think about making your children work at that age. I wasn't forced to work — I was asked and I accepted because there was money involved. I started baby-sitting the neighbor kids. After getting paid for the first time I wanted to baby-sit more, and so I did. Soon I had accumulated many clients.

One month before my sixteenth birthday I got a job at a Country Kitchen busing tables. When my birthday arrived, I began to wait on tables. I loved being a waitress. I met lots of people, made great tips, and had a lot of fun. Somewhere in that time I met my first husband. We started dating and about nine months later I got pregnant at the age of eighteen. That was not part of my plan. We were married eighteen months later, after my son was born. You cannot raise a child without money so I went back to being a waitress and paid for daycare as I worked. At the age of twenty I was pregnant again and had my second son. I stopped working as a waitress because it cost me more in daycare than I made.

A few months later I met a woman named Cathy who was a Tupperware director. I decided to have a Tupperware party and earn some Tupperware for myself, even though I was not planning on joining the business. I became so excited about all the wonderful things the business had to offer — in fact, they offered the opportunity to earn a new car. I went wild. When I told my parents what I had done, Dad said, "Why do you want to do that? You'll never make any money." I replied, "I'll show you I can."

One year from joining I earned my car. Talk about confidence and self esteem levels going up, I amazed even myself. Later, I learned how to leverage my confidence and improved self-esteem to create even greater success.

My relationship with my husband had always been rocky but by then it was worse. He drank a lot, did drugs, and never came home for his family. I found out later he was unfaithful. I left him a month before our third anniversary.

My aunt Alice took us in at that point. I left with nothing but clothes. I had no money, no food, and no car. One month later my kids and I moved out into an apartment. I applied for welfare and food stamps and got them. I knew I would never stay on welfare for a long period of time but it gave me time to think and focus on my kids.

I found the courage to go back to school and took a ten-month accounting course through a technical college just to get a degree and land a job. When I finished school I looked for jobs and ended up at a printing company making five dollars an hour — a humble salary for a single mother raising two children. It was tough for a while but as time went on I continued getting raises and eventually got off welfare.

Due to the turmoil in my life I have moved many times, and held several jobs. Although I did not always enjoy what I was doing, I made ends meet. Twenty-four years ago I met and married my current husband and have been happy ever since.

Throughout the years I explored and took risks I would never have done if I let another person hold me back from experiencing my own success. The challenges on my journey have led me to where I am today. One thing I was always sure of: I was never a failure — I was just one step closer to my goal in life.

I was not quite sure how to move forward until I discovered the Myers-Briggs test. I had five areas of interest: real estate, sales and marketing, beautician, insurance, and travel. I researched each of them to find the one that had the least amount of schooling. I ended up going to beauty school — I finally had a career. I became a licensed cosmetologist and worked at one of the top salons in Minnesota for thirteen years until a friend introduced me to a skin care and cosmetic company. Each time I was unsettled, I was at a crossroads looking for direction and purpose.

Today I can put the words to how I feel and who I am. As I look back I have found out a lot about myself. When I started, I was living in my challenges and suffered from a lack of self-esteem. I had no independence and lived day-to-day, paycheck-to-paycheck. Today I am a confident, creative leader, visionary, and CEO/owner of my own business. I have even become a speaker and an author.

Life throws us a lot of obstacles — it is up to us to figure out how to handle them. I am very proud of my accomplishments and the direction my life and career are taking me. I thank all the wonderful people in my life, most importantly my parents for giving me a solid work ethic combined with strong values.

Image Evolution Consulting, LLC is my business today. I work with women and men on finding their true passion. By exploring what drives them to do what they do, I help them move forward and conquer the world. We help our clients put into words who they are while enhancing the outer beauty to mirror the inner self. It is a holistic approach to uncovering the unique person you were always intended to be. The journey in life is all about evolving from where you are to where you want to be, and looking your best all around.

When you look good — you feel good. When you feel good — you perform better. When you perform better — good things come your way.

■ *Meet the Contributor*

DAWN STEBBING IS a fashion and beauty expert. She has over twenty-three years experience in the beauty industry and takes a holistic approach to helping her customers. She has discovered that personal style is only part of the beauty equation. True beauty is holistic: a combination of inner passion and outer styling to match. Through Image Evolution, Dawn helps clients discover their inner power and personal style so they can cultivate and harness their authentic beauty. Dawn is a licensed cosmetologist and graduate of Aveda Institute. She is a certified Leadership Coach, certified Core Passion facilitator, member of the Association of Image Consultants International, and a speaker and author. Contact Dawn at www.imageevolutionmn.com

Get Off Your Hamster Wheel — and Succeed

Tracie L. Church

THE NINE-TO-FIVE GRIND never fit me. I didn't know why, it just didn't. But I was taught the job mentality while growing up — go to work when you're sixteen until you finish high school, work your way through college, and find yet another job and stay on that hamster wheel until you retire.

Fast-forward to the digital age of 2007, and me being fired in a political power play at my job of eight years with a university research laboratory. I was an educated, intelligent, single mom of an eight-year-old daughter, receiving no child support and knowing I did not want to go back to a nine-to-five job, but not believing I could do anything else.

The initial thought I had on that first night of knowing I had no job to go to the next day was, "I've got good skills to offer. I've been making offices more efficient all my life and people are doing this online every day now." I had a beautiful child who depended on me for housing and food, and since she had no other parent to provide a good example, it was important I teach her how to get through anything life might throw at her.

I got online and started looking for another job, but this time with a different venue — my own home. I was getting closer to breaking through that old paradigm but I wasn't quite yet there. My online search brought me to a company contracting virtual assistants to their clients and I was able to apply without paying for any kind of certification or taking their online course.

The next day a friend who worked for herself as a real estate agent recommended I look into two part time sales positions that had just opened. This was outside my comfort zone, as I had never thought I was good at sales.

Both positions allowed me to create my own hours and put bread on the table, but what they really did was help me take a few more baby steps toward breaking free of my belief that a W-2 job was the only way to earn income. I stepped out of my comfort zone. I took a pay cut. But I also experienced the freedom of not paying for daycare, being with my daughter when she got home from school, having more time to make sure she completed her homework, and spending time with her before she went to bed. This freedom was more comfortable for me because I was able to: get up at an hour which was more in sync with my natural clock, work without someone looking over my shoulder or micro managing me, think creatively about how to deal with my clients, and leverage a team of like-minded people to share our collective ideas about how to bring in more business.

My mind opened a bit more and allowed me to start forming a vision of what I really wanted. Although one window of opportunity had closed when I lost my job, another more exciting window was opening.

Do you remember the virtual assistant company I had applied to? I had gotten my daughter to bed one evening and had just finished sending emails to sales clients. I stretched in my chair and said, "I am so thankful to have found these two positions so I can take care of my kiddo. I really enjoy this. However, I would really be grateful to put the skills I miss using to better use and show my daughter an example of making a living doing something you enjoy versus just going round and round on the hamster wheel." Before I shut my computer down, an email similar to several I had received each week for six months caught my eye.

It's amazing what comes to you once you open your mind and get specific about what you want. The email was for a position with the virtual assistant company I had applied to for a few hours a week doing exactly what I enjoy. I had worked three part time jobs while I attended college full time, so I knew I could work the two part time sales jobs and take on a few hours of contract work and not give up any of my newfound freedom. That window opened a bit further.

When I had enough virtual assistant contracts, I let one of the part time sales positions go: one W-2 down and one to go. I determined how much contract work I needed to bring in to let the other W-2 go. I had just set my first entrepreneurial goal.

I set out to find other ways of obtaining these contracts and used such sites as www.guru.com, www.elance.com, www.peopleperhour.com, and www.realpajamajobs.com. Another contract came from the virtual assistant company for fifteen hours a week as program director for one of Bob Proctor's programs. This contract changed my life in several ways; the client was not only a longtime serial entrepreneur but also a successful one.

This client had just taken an important step for an entrepreneur. He had gotten out of his way and grown his existing team by one more person to help him implement the things he needed done as part of his expanding business. One of my strengths was the ability to see what needed to be done and opening my mouth to start the conversation and the creative juices flowing to create the process of doing it. He grew because he contracted my services and I grew as I learned how entrepreneurial businesses are structured.

I was finally in my element. I left the last W-2 after two months of taking on the client. Work wasn't work any longer. It was a constant, inventive process of creating my own vision through helping my clients create their vision.

This fit me better than the daily grind. I worked within the skill sets I enjoyed and about which I was passionate, learned how to do it better every day, became more comfortable outside my comfort zone, and was constantly challenged.

That journey, which took almost a year, changed my mindset. I learned from my clients and recommended reading that successful entrepreneurs have a certain mindset, almost like that of a child. There is nothing they cannot do, no goal they cannot reach.

Visions and goals, however, are not enough. You must understand it is a process and work toward it, just as I was prepared to go out and find the contracts I needed to walk away from my W-2 and work my tail off at both the W-2 and obtaining new contract work. You must actively seek out the people who can provide the information you need.

One of my clients was a master business coach for Loral Langemeier's Live Out Loud. I asked him questions all the time and learned from every call. I attended free and paid webinar classes for best practices in the virtual assistant industry, where I learned what to charge for my services, how to get new clients, and what boundaries to set before entering into a contract. I started to narrow my niche as I learned new things and determined not only what I was best at, but also what I really enjoyed doing in the industry.

My virtual assistance business began with me "working" (in my own mind) for another virtual assistant company. I set my own hours, but I still had job mentality. Once I changed my mindset, I realized what I was worth and asked for it from a few independent individuals. I also realized just how much I could help entrepreneurs grow and it felt good to see how my passion for making business processes more efficient and dealing with customers as I had throughout my career was much more useful for these individuals than in the corporate world.

Once I surrounded myself with people who supported my idea of having my own business and enjoying my daughter's life before she was grown and gone, I actively sought out new clients and added new team members to take on those clients.

Coaches and mentors helped me remove the clutter in order to identify the goals I wanted to set. I took the steps they recommended to solidify my business and prepare it for growth. And grow it has.

The one word my friends, family, and former employers use to describe me is "resourceful." If I don't know how to do something I will learn or find someone who does know to teach me or just handle it. When my mindset was finally where it needed to be, my resourcefulness and the ability to use it was boundless. This remains the most valuable tool in my success toolbox.

The business and life of an entrepreneur is ever changing. This is the only thing about an entrepreneurial business that remains constant: it can grow as big as you envision it. What must not change is your faith in yourself to roll, flow, and grow with the changes that come along in your personal and entrepreneurial life. To be successful, you need to unlock your resourcefulness to find the mentors, team members, processes, services, and answers you need for your business to always step to the next level, whether you're just starting out as an entrepreneur or if you've been in business for yourself for decades.

Meet the Contributor

TRACIE L. CHURCH is a graduate of the University of Science and Arts of Oklahoma, with a BS in history (her first passion). She has twenty-seven years of experience as an executive assistant, office manager, and travel agent. She has lived in Oklahoma, Grand Cayman, Jacksonville, Florida, Elizabeth City, North Carolina, and finally returned to Oklahoma to raise her daughter close to her family. Contact Tracie at www.tlcvirtualassistants.com

APPLYING THE
LESSONS OF MOTHERHOOD

Gwena Morrill (LBT #74)

I DIDN'T ALWAYS smile. There were days when my very existence seemed squeezed to the limit. No matter how hard I tried, my best was not good enough. Yet, I was committed and I went on and I made it. I didn't attain all I wanted, but I'm still alive. I have a happy although very busy and often stressful life. And I can smile.

In response to a recent family newsletter one of my daughters sent me this email: "My oh my! You need to write a new book and sell it on eBay. You could have a wild tale just about the happenings in your own family. This makes soap operas look boring. But most of all you could inspire people about how to hold up and stay sane in the middle of insanity."

She was referring mostly to situations and happenings in our family. As I thought about the challenges we've had, the strategies and the tactics we used to bring about solutions are not all that different from those necessary to be an entrepreneur. In fact, many of the principles involved are the same.

My husband Stan and I had two daughters, but wanted more children. We took in several foster children but really wanted to adopt so that they didn't just come and go. Eventually we adopted two of our long-term foster children, a boy and a girl. About the same time we adopted a baby boy. Deciding we wanted one more boy, we applied once again.

However, instead of getting one boy, we ended up with three boys and four girls — brothers and sisters who wanted to stay together.

Suddenly we were a family with twelve children, from one to ten years old. Some people called us brave; others said we were crazy. The situation we found ourselves in is not so different from starting your own business. Considering the challenges involved, there is a fine line between playing it safe and staying where you are versus gathering up your courage and stepping up to try something new. Here are some of the lessons we learned.

Lesson #1: Before you begin any new adventure, whether it be a big family or starting a new business, you need to have a plan, one or more goals, and you have to consider the cost in time, energy, finances, and emotions. What is it going to take to be successful?

Before we adopted the seven children, we made a list of everything we could think of that would affect us, including everything that could go wrong. The list of things that could go wrong took up about three-quarters of a single-spaced page. The reality was about three times that long. We had kids run away from home, drop out of school, and put sand into the gas tank of the neighbor's tractor. At one point all seven got into alcohol and/or drugs. One still has a major problem. We've had boys in jail and girls with mental illness. Several of our children had to deal with sexual assault — some before we got them and some afterwards. Everyone felt discrimination in one form or another. We added counselor, mediator, arbitrator, disciplinarian, and advocate to our roles.

Lesson #2: When you begin a business, you have to know your goal or goals, and as much as possible about what to plan for, what to expect, and what roles you need to play.

An immediate and constant challenge we faced was to integrate the old family with the new. With our first five children, we were connected and together. Merging with seven strangers didn't come easy. For a long time it was an "us" and "them" organization. Bringing them together took lots of leadership and teamwork. Stan and I had to have the same goals and values and remain united in our leadership. We had to agree on strategies and tactics and be united in how we worked with everyone in the family to bring about the results we wanted.

Lesson #3: Just like our family, a business has to have a team and teamwork in order to become successful. Everyone on the team must have the same values and work toward the same goal, yet be able to express their differences. At the same time it is important that each team member understands his or her role in the business. Rules, policies, and procedures need to be clearly defined so there are no misunderstandings and everyone knows what is expected of them.

In our family we learned to work as a council. Stan and I had "parent planning meetings" where we discussed needs and problems. After the two of us reached agreement, we took the situation to a family council to get the input from everyone in the family. We encouraged everyone to give their ideas and we'd discuss them. When decisions were made, we wrote out detailed instructions about everything in order that everyone understood. It's rare for a business to be just one person. At some point, it will grow — and there has to be an integration of everyone involved.

Lesson #4: When you create a business, it is extremely important to know everything you can about the business before you start. Know everything about what to expect, even the daily routine. This is a small glimpse of life in a family with twelve children:

- Trying to read the newspaper after six schoolers have been looking for current events

- Having a big birthday party without inviting anyone

- Everyone having a best friend — who lived in

- Running your own restaurant, beauty salon, barber shop, bakery, taxi service, laundry, first aid station, and counseling service

- Searching for peace and quiet with nine kids taking piano lessons

- Saying, "Lights out" at a slumber party

- Having the full Sunday School program even when you're snowed in

- Forty-four school lunches every week still isn't enough

- Making 135 peanut butter sandwiches every week

- Going home with a busload of kids and finding out they're all yours

- Taking two days to attend parent teacher conferences and the next two days for conferences with the kids

- Going Christmas shopping with two kids — six times

- Constantly teaching life skills, piano lessons, gardening, resource management, and how to get along with each other

Lesson #5: Every business will have elements that will give you a headache and make you tired. Be prepared. Do everything you can to stay fit and healthy. There will be events in every business venture that are not anticipated and will take a toll on your emotional wellbeing. Plan for it.

The physical challenges made my head spin, my back ache, and my stomach cramp. I went to the doctor to see why I was so fatigued. After giving me a thorough exam, he declared, "You're tired." And the emotional drain was even harder.

Lesson #6: Financial management is vital to any business. Start up money can be hard to find. Learn how money works and how you will use it. Planning and forecasting are essential to starting and maintaining a successful business.

Our finances were really tight. The adoptions were finalized in 1973 just before the big energy crisis hit, prices skyrocketed, and interest rates went through the roof. Stan was an educator; I worked part time at an assortment of jobs when I could. We weren't always sure where we'd get the money for the next jug of milk or the next pair of shoes. I learned to pinch every penny and stretch every dollar. We made a plan and used our resources wisely.

Lesson #7: Time for recreation and relaxation are also important in a business. Don't neglect it.

Family activities were an important part of our life. We took some kind of vacation every year. We also camped, hiked, swam, played tennis, softball, basketball, and other activities. We even went to a movie once in awhile.

I learned a lot of things in raising my family (many of which I wished I'd never had to learn). All those experiences have made me the person I am today. And I am a success. I am not rich, but I learned to manage well enough that we've lived in nice houses, driven nice cars, and Stan and I have traveled much of the world. Our wealth was created in so many other ways: we created a family business when the kids were living at home so they could learn how to earn and to have their own spending money. I never made "Mother of the Year" — that's always decided by the significant, notable accomplishments of the children as judged by the ways of the world. But we are all still a family, and all the kids call us Mom and Dad and keep in touch. I never became famous because I could sing or act. But I learned how to survive when times were tough. I learned how to organize and improvise.

Things I could not control often made me feel like a failure, but I learned to believe in myself. The only person I can control is myself, and my happiness depends on what I do and how I think, not on the ideas and behavior of someone else. I set goals and work toward them. In many cases I learned to redefine success. And I've learned to be flexible enough to change my strategies and tactics when necessary. As you look at your own business, ask yourself what lessons you have learned (or been unwilling to face). Ask yourself, "How can I redefine my own success?"

I made a commitment. With lots of encouragement from Stan, friends, and my faith in God, I kept going. It has been insane, but I am a success.

And I still smile.

▪ *Meet the Contributor*

GWENA MORRILL IS a mother of twelve children, ten of which are adopted. From oldest to youngest they are only nine years apart. Now that the children are all on their own, Gwena realizes many of the lessons she learned as a mother also apply to meeting the challenges of becoming a successful entrepreneur. It takes belief in yourself, planning, goal setting, team work, understanding, preparation, management, perseverance, and a healthy mental attitude. Gwena is the author of *How to Get More Food for Your Money*, which is currently being revised and updated. She has also written a calendar-type book called, *Money Rules From Grandma Jewel*. Currently, Gwen works with Financial $olutions providing financial education, strategies, and solutions to help businesses and families succeed financially.

Contact Gwena at www.moneyrulesandmore.com

MORE PASSION MORE WEALTH

Shivani Gupta (LBT #73)

YOU CAN EARN a lot of money and still not feel content. However, by putting PASSION into your wealth creation, it will be easier and more fulfilling.

I was earning good money in my corporate career but after a life changing trip to Nepal, I realized I was unhappy and generating that wealth was getting harder and harder. However, now that I'm being true to my PASSION, wealth creation is easier and more enjoyable. Here is my formula:

▦ P IS FOR PURPOSE

HAVE YOU HAD times in your life when you wonder what you are here to do, when you have questioned your purpose? What is the legacy you want to leave behind? Why are you here? What do you want to do? If money were no object, what would you do? How would you make a difference? These are the questions you need to answer to uncover your purpose.

I was driven from an early age and when I got to a senior management role with a globally leading company at twenty-seven, I thought I had achieved my purpose. However, when I got to Nepal, I experienced life so simply, it made me realize I had acquired my material possessions in a way that was not making me happy.

One day a beautiful little boy of five, whose face I still see when I close my eyes, came up to me. I lowered my backpack and took out a lolly (sweet) and gave it to him. Then his three-year-old sister followed. I thought, "she'll ask me for a lolly too," but she didn't. She just stood there and smiled at her brother. As if he did it every day, without conscious thought, he bit his lolly and gave his sister half. He put the other half in the wrapper and stuck it in his pocket. He smiled as if I'd just given him a million dollars. I cried. In that moment I wanted what he had. I had more material things but did not have his contentment. That day I decided I wanted to create my wealth by unlocking peoples' passion. So many people don't take the opportunity to be their true, authentic self — to be true to their passion and purpose.

When do you take the time to find your Nepal? When do you reflect on what you've been thinking about doing for a long time? If you take a step forward toward knowing your purpose, wealth creation is easier because you are doing what you love.

A IS FOR ASSOCIATIONS

To be successful it is important to be around people that have a positive attitude most of the time. When you are around negative people, their energy rubs off. Take responsibility for the key associations in your life, including those that aren't working.

You also need balanced associations. Sometimes we only want to see how amazing people are and none of their downsides. Other times we see people negatively and never look at their good points.

If someone has made you angry, think about what they do well. Ask why you have difficult people in your life and what are they teaching you. Make sure that by putting someone on a pedestal or in the clouds you don't indirectly put yourself down. I put Oprah up in the clouds but I look at the things I like about her, like inspiring others and being philanthropic, and tell myself I can also do these things, although on a smaller scale, so I feel like an equal.

I've had people in my life that I disliked. To ensure that negative energy does not stop me from achieving my purpose and passion I look at the things they do well — if not toward me, then toward others.

Think about a person you dislike and say out loud one thing they do well or one good quality they have. (Don't grind your teeth as you do it, otherwise you'll need to visit the dentist.)

The other point about balanced associations is that you will never be happy all the time. Look for balance in your life and choose to find the good in people.

▪ S IS FOR STRENGTH

MAKE YOUR MIND strong with affirmations and meditation. These important tools can help you change your behavior and allow you time to think clearly about the big picture and wealth creation opportunities.

Make your body strong with regular exercise and a good diet to ensure you are fit and well to take on opportunities and enjoy the benefits. Use the Pareto principle: eat well eighty percent of the time. That allows you to splurge on four out of twenty-one meals a week.

My grandfather and amazing mentor passed away last year at the age of eighty-five in India. He was the healthiest person in my family. He walked every morning and balanced his eating — if he overate in one meal, he would cut down the next. He prayed and meditated every day ensuring he was very strong in his mind. When he decided to do something, nothing got in his way, even if his own children disapproved. He was an inspiration. He came from humble beginnings in a poor family. He always said one of the best things about having money was it allowed you to eat well and live well. Have the strength to enjoy your wealth.

Find a form of exercise you enjoy. I dragged myself to the gym for years, sticking to it only because I knew not doing anything was not good. Then I found yoga. By being true to my passion I find it easy to exercise and am much happier when I am doing it.

What do you do to exercise your mind and body? Do you want to dance at your child's or grandchild's wedding or use a walker? Get clear on how long you want to live, how well you want to live, and how your brain will be functioning when you pass. A strong body and mind will help you unlock your passion, enjoy it for longer, and create more wealth in the process.

■ S is for Style

UNDERSTANDING YOUR OWN and other people's style are important for connecting with people to help you to achieve your wealth creation goals. People often say to me they have been born a certain way (being introverted or extroverted) and that is just their style. This is not true. For most people, when there is a topic they are passionate about, they become extroverted. When there is a topic they are not interested in, they are introverted. If you talk to me about diapers on sale, I am pretty introverted. Talk to me about a seminar with amazing speakers, I get excited and extroverted. Realize what your passions are and how your style comes across with different people and conversations.

Style is also about your personality traits. Whether you use Myers-Briggs, LSI, or the birds model (approximately fifteen types around the world), they will indicate your strengths and weaknesses. Become aware of them. Enhance your strengths and combat your weaknesses.

■ I is for Investment

MONEY GIVES YOU choices. When you have money you create experiences. Timothy Ferriss, author of the bestseller, *The 4-Hour Workweek*, said, "it's not that we want to have a million dollars in the bank, we want to experience what millionaires experience." This may be taking your family on a special holiday, going to a course, or giving money to a charity you are passionate about. To build wealth you need to learn about money. You may need to change your belief systems about money. Visualize more income in your life and get clear on what you will do with that money once you have it.

One of the beliefs I grew up with was you have to work hard for your money. This is absolutely not true. Money is easy and comes easily. You just have to know you deserve it. When I got paid fifty dollars for my first speaking engagement eight years ago, I felt it was too much considering I did something I love to do. Now I command (rather than demand) thousands of dollars because I know I own that space and what I deliver is worth that to people. To allow wealth generation to occur you need to be clear on your space. You need to consciously think about and work out how to generate more money, and negotiate more income in your life.

The best work in this field I have come across is by Loral. As a result of investing in myself and learning how to make money, I generated another $100,000 of sales in the month after doing my first session of the Big Table.

O IS FOR OPEN MIND

OPEN YOUR MIND to the three-D principle. When faced with any task I ask if I can *delete* it. If not, can I *delegate* it? If I can't do either, then the last D is for *do.*

Deleting includes saying no to things you don't want to do but do out of obligation. Say no to opportunities that are not in alignment with your passion. Delegate reminds you it is okay to get some help. Stop trying to do every thing yourself and ask for help.

Which leaves us with the third D. Anything not deleted or delegated must be done. Work on your most important things first. Apply this to emails, projects, and everything. Get organized. Stop procrastinating on what you must do. Have that performance discussion with some-one who is causing lots of issues in the team. Market your team to get more resources allocated to your division. Get organized. Take care of anything that needs to be done as quickly as possible. What is one thing you could do this week to move closer to your goal? Decide to accomplish that task and find an accountability partner who can hold you responsible. Become present with what you do. Prioritize — when the baby is crying, he or she comes first. Cleaning your mind creates more space for creative work and will make you more money.

N IS FOR NICHE

BEING A GENERALIST does not cut it. The division of labor was created in our capitalist system for a very good reason. Successful people and companies know their unique selling proposition or niche. Your niche is your passion. Become a master in what you do. Reading for one hour a day on your subject of choice will make you a master in that area within three to five years. There are only 4,000 weeks in one lifetime, so work out where you are on that timeline and what you want to be known for as an expert.

This niche is based on your passion and because it is, being the best in your area of expertise inspires you.

▪ *Meet the Contributor*

SHIVANI GUPTA IS an expert on passion. Through her thriving coaching business, Passionate People Institute, she has helped thousands of people to unlock their passion to lead more fulfilling lives, be better leaders, and have more successful businesses.

She was born in India and grew up in Australia. A qualified engineer, she completed an MBA in her mid-twenties before working as a senior executive for a major company. After a life-changing trip to Nepal after 9/11, she found her true passion, quit the corporate world, and established her own business. She works with individuals, sole traders, and some of Australia's top companies. Her expertise has won her a number of awards including "Telstra Young Business Woman of the Year."

Shivani's journey from corporate warrior to business butterfly is told in her book, *Passion @ Work*, which has also been published in Mandarin. She is also a columnist for *Fairfax*, one of Australia's major newspapers. In 2008 she hosted a TV series, coaching start up small businesses, which screened on the Australia's national SBS network. A big advocate of work-life balance, she has also produced a CD — *Meditation for Busy People*.

Shivani is a Certified Speaking Professional (CSP), the highest designation awarded internationally to professional speakers. As well as running her own business, Shivani is a mother of two young children and stepmother of two teenage children.

Contact Shivani at www.passionatepeopleinstitute.com

Living by Design

PaTrisha-Anne Todd

"You can do it, PaTrisha-Anne — go and get your dream."

Mum was no ordinary lady. She was true, full of grace, and exuded beauty with a *je ne sais quoi* that made her stand out from the crowd. Bless you, Mum, and sleep in peace without pain. Thankfully her main trait of determination has filtered through to me.

It is with gratitude in my heart that I share how as an ordinary person I've had the privilege to become an entrepreneur. Entrepreneurialism is working for yourself and taking the time to help others do the same. I love it, and not surprisingly being an independent female, living and celebrating entrepreneurship fits my lifestyle like a glove.

My apprenticeship began in the early 1950s when Mum and Dad decided as young lovers with fire in their hearts to try their hand at living a new life in England. Separately in 1951, within months of each other they sailed from India to the UK. They married and in 1952 I arrived to post-war Britain: food and clothing coupons, and old money — pounds, shillings, and pence. Mum kept our home while Dad began his musical career as a bandleader by night and writing orchestrations by day, a real entrepreneur rising from nothing to something.

Over half a century later as a mature baby boomer, I live the same journey of entrepreneurship my parents took all those years before. There is nothing as exhilarating as being in the company of dynamic people who are specific in their choice of living and working. Today I write books and mentor like-minded dynamic individuals to live life on purpose.

There is no secret to success, and yet some people struggle needlessly in their lives. The only action that gives consistent power is application to working the business, step-by-step with smart goal planning and focused purpose. I teach this approach to life to the individuals who want to be more, have more, and do more. They are entrepreneurs-in-training who know they want to make a difference in their own life and give back to the community. My teaching style is step-by-step. I created a powerful, instant-results system to use in all areas of life. This six-step success system reveals the fundamentals involved with earning more money while working from home as an independent business owner or direct sales agent (versus being a contributor to the rat race, employed but limited and miserable). I know how to bring people to purpose and reach their potential while earning a substantial income.

■ THREE ELEMENTS THAT CREATE SUCCESS AS AN ENTREPRENEUR

KNOWING THE ENTREPRENEURIAL strategies that create business success makes a difference, no matter if the business is at a founding stage or moving toward expansion.

Many times I've reminded my coaching clients about the theory that if you aim at nothing you'll hit it — nothing. The big fat zero leaves you empty, disappointed, and miserable. That is not a place I recommend. Sadly, lots of people choose to sit on the couch and let opportunity and life drift away. What a shame that in the twenty-first century so many people do that. This is why it's part of my life's mission to educate and motivate as many people as I can to step up and out of their comfort zone to become business owners.

To avoid missing your goal, there are three parts to the success building cycle my mentor and coaches have helped me identify and utilize on my special voyage:

1. Subconscious and conscious mindsets have an enormous impact on the human behavior patterns that form a strong, positive mindset with an attitude of gratitude. What I mean by an attitude of gratitude refers to the universal laws of metaphysics, a natural science based on positive thinking and focused action for the higher good. Within your daily lifestyle, express gratitude for what you have come to know. This is a part of the natural cycle of gratitude.

2. Eliminate self sabotage and harness the principles of the Laws of Attraction, again another universal law that states you attract what you put your attention on. Have you noticed that when you think about somebody, within hours you meet them in the street, receive a phone call from them, or someone else mentions them?

3. Practice Extreme Self Care both mentally and physically. This plays a huge role in feeling good and looking good with grace and elegance, regardless of any disability or financial challenges. Extreme Self Care is a concept I created that teaches people how to Live Life by Design.

Every success begins with a dream. Take your dream and feed it by working diligently toward achieving your goals.

▨ LIFE HAS LOWS AND HIGHS, AND I'VE HAD MY SHARE

HAVING A CLEAR vision of my goals with a desire to achieve my dreams has always been a part of my strategy, coupled with a step-by-step plan backed up with consistency and big thinking.

Every day I demonstrate proactive leadership by focusing my efforts on the core of my goals plan. I work on the elements I can do something about and find other people, perhaps team members, to take care of the rest. This is how I work.

I make it my business to acknowledge, mix, and work with other upbeat, positive, and energetic people so I can improve my technique and enlarge and increase my business base. This is pure nectar, giving me the motivation to feed my reason for living and keeping me on purpose. I am focused and continually moving forward to my goals. Give this technique a try. I promise you'll be raring to go and surprised once you become one hundred percent conscious at how easy goal achievement can be.

This thinking has helped me overcome some of the struggles life has presented me with: acute lung disease, chronic back pain, single parenthood, degenerative muscle disease, financial hardship, and bereavement. Having a positive mental attitude has ensured I never lose my focus and vision for my personal existence and, more importantly, my family.

Anyone can become an entrepreneur if they have a broad enough scope to apply themselves to making a success of their business project. Being an entrepreneur requires a mix of talent, skills set, determination, ambition, integrity, honesty, networking proficiency, good business sense, financial know how, tip-top delegation tactics, and the desire to succeed. Luckily, being an entrepreneur does not have to be a sole exercise. Ideally, it is implemented as a team effort, which helps to leverage both speed to market and the generation of cash flow.

▐ MAKE AN IMPACT ON OTHERS

A CONVERSATION I had several years ago with a personal development teacher about inertia holding back progress and how to create a complete and full lifestyle led me to several secrets for creating more joy and success in life. I took away with me the knowledge that life requires daily application to keep on track, generate wealth, and support those in need. I have since incorporated those teachings into my core being. Doing this has made an enormous difference in my personal life and business projects.

▐ CAN I REALLY MAKE MY DREAMS COME TRUE?

YES, YOU CAN. Everyone has the potential to become more than they currently are. Whether they rise to the opportunity or not is up to them. For myself, I choose to stretch so that I create more abundance and prosperity in my life. I learned by honing my communication skills I could attract the right kind of conversations with intelligent and wise people who are always keen to share their knowledge and wit. It's music to my ears when I can converse with another who thinks like me. The art of conversation is not dead; it has turned me into a people magnet.

Deciding to make positive changes is powerful especially when a situation that doesn't work needs to be dealt with. For example, deciding today to apply forward-moving strategies can change your present circumstances and move you closer to your goals much faster than you ever thought possible. I make choices deliberately — it's a habit I've gotten into. I decide if and when change needs to happen. Thankfully, I have my mentor coach to keep me accountable to my dreams and reality.

Another secret is networking, and the Laws of Attraction help with this exercise. Networking boosts confidence levels and adds more power to life. I know this for a fact and encourage you to adopt the craft of networking for building relationships.

Finally, there is the amazing secret of being aware of the rules about money. Money is a fabulous bartering tool; it's full of energy and when used wisely and respectfully gives stunning returns.

I wholeheartedly endorse the idea of working as an entrepreneur for money. The universe attracts entrepreneurs to make even more money for all of us. Go for life in a big way: enjoy being an entrepreneur and Live Life by Design.

▉ *Meet the Contributor*

PaTrisha-Anne Todd, LCSi, author, speaker, founder of Life Coach School international, creator of Coaching Kinetics and the Six-Step Coaching Model, and coaching consultant to executives and entrepreneurs. "Dynamic, inspiring, and strategic coaching" is how clients describe PaTrisha-Anne Todd in her results-focused Live Life by Design programs.

She is especially qualified to coach motivated career seekers and entrepreneurs who expect only the best resources to achieve the outcomes they want. She works with clients via Internet, telephone, and face-to-face around the world by appointment.

PaTrisha-Anne broadcasts weekly international coaching casts on-line and is a guest expert on BBC Radio. Keynote talks, personal development articles, and research for her books keeps her busy. She lives in the south of England with her family and pets. Contact PaTrisha-Anne at www.patrishaanne.com or www.lifecoachschoolinternational.co.uk

Changing Your Results

It's a Matter of Perspective

Linda Wilson

I HAD BEEN doing this my whole life, but I had no idea what I was doing. Do you ever feel like you have no idea how you get from one place to the next, or one step to the next but you just keep going? We've all felt that way at one time or another. I felt that way for over forty years.

I grew up a loser. I was so pathetic even I didn't like me. I had no friends and was helpless to explain why no one liked me. I was destined to live an unremarkable life. However, I started to change without realizing it. I began to stand up for myself, and things that mattered to me. It didn't make a difference if people agreed with me or not. I knew it was the right thing to do.

▉ THE BEGINNING

I WAS RAISED Catholic, very Catholic. My grandmother went to church every day. She knew Mother Theresa. My aunt was a nun in Mother Theresa's order and traveled with her. I went to Catholic schools from second grade on, including an all-girl Catholic high school.

But the loser that I was, I got pregnant just after high school. I married my boyfriend, Jeff, who was an atheist. That went over well. I married against my parent's wishes. I was underage and my father threatened to withhold consent. So I told him I'd move in with Jeff until I was of age, and then marry him. He consented, but wasn't going to attend the wedding (it wasn't in a church). I told him that was his choice but if he didn't come to the wedding, he wouldn't know his first grandchild. So he came. And he celebrated and rejoiced. Although I couldn't believe I stood up for us that way, I substantially changed our results.

Several years later my husband needed surgery. The surgeons couldn't agree on what they needed to do, and when my husband signed the consent form, I discovered it was going to be a different surgery than what they had originally told him. So I called our family physician and put a stop to it before they wheeled him into the operating room. My mother (a nurse) thought I was insane: you can't tell a doctor no. Oh, yes I can. I knew Jeff would be furious if he woke up and learned the surgery was one he did not want. What's a wife to do?

▪ ATTITUDE AND PERSPECTIVE

JEFF AND I moved to a new town where we didn't know anyone. I realized no one knew me, or what a loser I was. No one would know I was faking being a normal person. I got to start fresh and new.

The next ten years represented a period where the accomplishments were never-ending and always increasing. Even as I did them and got the results I wanted, I didn't understand. I didn't know I was doing anything special, or why every once in awhile I'd come out on top. I didn't get it at first. An inkling of the truth began to reveal itself: even as the obstacles became larger and larger, I continued to get the results I desired.

My husband and I have been gone from our hometown for over twenty years. Since we don't see our relatives that often, my family forgets I'm not the loser I was when I was younger. Whenever we return home, I'm always a surprise to them.

I was forty-six before I learned and understood that attitude affects everything; by changing my perspective and outlook on things, I made things better. For example, I was in a job I didn't like, surrounded by negativity, and starting to drown in everyone else's depression. I overcame these circumstances — the same that you may be facing in your life.

My passion is photography, and once I started studying it, I saw that many of the things I do to get better photographs were the same things I did to get a better life. I did it without thinking whenever I picked up a camera, but I didn't see how it worked in my life as well.

Once I understood that, I left my job and went into business as a professional photographer. I'm a great photographer, and it was about time I realized it and put my heart and soul into what I had been doing my whole life.

Not only did I realize my passion for photography, it became an insistent dream to stop everything else and focus on a life behind the camera, capturing beauty and wonder, to share with all. I dreamed of my studio (still in progress but closer every day) and see everything with a photographer's eye. I notice color, detail, and things I thought everyone saw but they don't.

I work for myself in my photography business and never been happier. My camera is always with me, waiting to capture an amazing moment. When I take nature photos, I lose myself in the surroundings, and sometimes don't realize what fabulous photos I've taken until I get back to the house or the hotel. I've been blessed with an amazing gift and more blessed to be able to share it with others.

Someone asked me what I would do if I weren't in my present line of work. My response was clear: "I would go stir crazy, as I'm now living my passion. There is no other option for me."

My life and business continue to attract success. I get to travel and take amazing photos. I talk to groups and organizations on how photography mirrors business and life: you change your focus or perspective, and the result changes. I had been doing that for years in photography and didn't realize it worked in life as well. That realization has helped me greatly as I proceed on my journey. I also share this with others to help them on their journey.

▇ THE POWER OF MENTORING

To GET FROM there to here, I found several mentors over the years. I followed what they told me to do, and my heart. When you do what you love, even just a little, it gives you confidence and fulfillment. I depended on that when I was still in my job. It got me through the tough times, helped me remember why I was working toward my goal, and how important it was to me. If photography hadn't gotten me through all that, then it would not have been my purpose, my passion, and reason for breathing.

I have met and worked with some of the most amazing people: Mother Theresa, Bob Proctor, Paul Martinelli, Les Brown, Orrin Hudson, Gerry Robert, Cynthia Ulmer, and my husband, Jeff. All these individuals gave me faith in myself and showed me how to stay true to my dream, the dream I didn't know I had.

I hope that you find the activity that makes you feel alive. We all have one. Find yours and pursue it with everything you've got. It's what you're here for. Don't keep it from yourself or all of us. Don't let it slip away.

▇ *Meet the Contributor*

LINDA M. WILSON is a professional photographer with multiple areas of focus, and a public speaker. She has mentored with Bob Proctor, Gerry Robert, Paul Martinelli, and Les Brown. In 2009 she took a leap of faith and quit her job to start her photography business. Linda's passion for nature photography and people shows in her photographs. She and Jeff, her husband of thirty-one years, have lived in Denver for sixteen years and call it home. Contact Linda at www.yourworldourlens.com

Breaking Free of
The Black Curtain

Christine Heart Savage

The thought shocked me as I walked past him in the corridor, "He's going to be my husband." It was the first day in my new job. I hadn't met the man; it was a blink in time and he was gone.

It was like I'd always loved him when I saw him. We finally met a year later at a conference in an elegant resort. The weather was wonderful, the change of scenery was welcome, and he was charming.

Two years passed and the next conference was approaching. Deep within me I knew something powerful was about to happen. With a strange feeling in my stomach I packed my bags for the impending adventure. I was consumed with nervous excitement as I approached my destination. Again the resort was warm, opulent, and luxurious. My surroundings opposed my single mother status and lifestyle; even the weather contradicted my normal reality.

I breathed in every delicious particle of the new resort home as I found my way to my room, and there he was. Our eyes met.

At dinner that night, every glance sent vibes zapping across the room, their magnetic force paralyzing me. In the following days the air was electric with a magic I'd never known. Every nerve in my body was alive and danced the song of love through my being. For five days and six nights we talked. On the last evening he asked me to consider moving in with him. Wow, but impossible, I thought.

Departure morning came around swiftly. I gave him a quick hug and left on the bus for the airport with my fellow travelers, bound for home and a life that was never to be the same. We married three months later and moved interstate. That's when it all began. I loved this man and tried so hard to make it work. But it was a living hell.

His personality oscillated between cries of forgiveness and abusive attacks. In company he was always Mister Charming and everyone loved him. I had married Dr. Jekyll and Mr. Hyde and I didn't know which one would arrive home at the end of the day. Stress and anxiety feasted on my body.

He hardly spoke, and when he did, venom poured from his lips. His violent, irrational moods took their toll on the children and me. For the last twelve months we lived together he put up a black curtain and separated himself from the family. The black curtain became a symbol of dread. He was messing with my mind. I was losing myself.

Disoriented, emotionally decayed, and exhausted, I ended the torture we were living. I knew I would die if I stayed. My body ached, my mind screamed, and my heart was shattered. I had a choice to make. I chose me. I chose life.

▓ THE RESURRECTION BEGINS

I DIVORCED MY husband, sold my home, and resigned from my demanding job. The children and I moved into a small rented house close to the beach. I didn't want medication or hospitalization but I knew I had to clear the black curtain in my soul.

▓ DEALING WITH THE AFTERMATH

MY DAUGHTER FOUND companionship in drugs to escape her pain and battled with addiction for more than ten years. Although my son seemed to handle the stress better, he was later found to have a tumor-like growth in his brain that caused hemorrhages and epileptic seizures. He was also diagnosed with Multiple Sclerosis.

Whether or not these issues were a direct cause of the war zone we'd lived in, I can't say. I do know we were not equipped with the stress management or life skills to help us cope with the trauma we'd experienced.

▮ THE FIRST STEP TO HEALING... MY INITIATION INTO MEDITATION

THERE WERE THE two of us in the small room, strangers sharing an intimate moment. I placed the flowers and fruit I was requested to bring on the modest altar, and sat not knowing what to expect. The scene was foreign to me and I was apprehensive, and yet there was an underlying feeling encouraging me to continue. I sat with closed eyes in a space that felt awkward and unfamiliar.

I repeated the mantra (words) given to me by my teacher. Within seconds a strange hum started moving through my body. I could feel something taking place inside, as if my cells were awakening, like they had jumped up together and started dancing to the same tune. A pulsating sensation charged through my body. Every part was buzzing in unison. I became an illuminated, harmonious symphony. I felt electrified as I sat in reverent silence; but this was no ordinary silence — this silence was alive. It roared.

A deep sense of recognition welled within, an immense, inexplicable feeling of what I can only describe as love, permeated me. In this moment I knew I had come home. At last, I was home. It was as if every longing, every question I had ever asked, was answered in this moment. I had found truth.

A Child of the "Light"

Let me feel your presence
Fill me with your light

Let me feel your numbing hum
Begin to power me
As you suck away my breath
and fill me with your nectar

For I am one...

Expand me through your brilliance
Burst my heart with beauty
Stream my eyes with joy
Blind me with your love

For I am one...

Encumber me and dwell in me
Your radiance I feel
Your ocean welcomes me — just be
To dip in it I plea

For I am one
A child of the light...

I retreated from the world for seven months and sat in meditation for many hours each day. I made progress on my journey to wellness. My son practiced meditation, too.

I was reminded of the words of Jesus Christ, one of the world's greatest masters and life coaches, who asked, "What shall it profit a man if he gains the whole world but loses his soul?"

▨ TAKING THE REINS AND STARTING MY OWN BUSINESS

IN 1994 I started my personal development business. I was passionate about helping other people. I studied different modalities over many years and integrated them into my work. I became a breathwork therapist and national breathwork trainer. "Breathing" became a very important part of my life. I breathed my way to freedom and empowerment.

Stress and breathing are intricately related. When you are stressed your breathing is affected. When you become a skilled breather, stress cannot build up in the body/mind. You can breathe your way to balance and health.

My past was a gift, and this is the lesson I want to transfer to you. I drew not only from my studies but also from my life experience to teach life skills and stress recovery programs. I have run hundreds of groups, seminars, and workshops and seen over seven thousand private clinical clients, with wonderful results. I have found my purpose and I love my work. My daily discipline of breathing and meditation keeps me balanced, strong, and well.

In the depth of darkness and despair, don't give up. Go within and find the doorway that leads to freedom. It is there, I promise you.

When you combine life skills, breathwork therapy, breath awareness, and meditation, you can't help but become balanced, non-attached, peaceful, and well. Personal empowerment, self-awareness, and a deeper knowledge of life emerge with these practices. But the most important thing is that you come home to yourself.

That leaves you with a challenge: What experiences of your own can you take advantage of today to start a successful business this year?

The power is within. My soul is my anchor, my stillness, and my truth. No matter what is done to me, nobody can take my soul. I learned to honor and love myself, to trust myself and surrender to life. These lessons always support me in amazing ways.

I have such gratitude for the experiences of my life. Through adversity I found the greatest treasure house in the universe. With my business and beloved children, each of who are successful in their own areas of expertise, I am rich beyond words. I found my soul.

My favorite poem by Mary Stevenson says it all. It always makes me misty-eyed.

Footprints in the Sand

One night I dreamed I was walking along the beach with the Lord.
Many scenes from my life flashed across the sky.
In each scene I noticed footprints in the sand.
Sometimes there were two sets of footprints,
other times there were one set of footprints.

This bothered me because I noticed
that during the low periods of my life,
when I was suffering from
anguish, sorrow or defeat,
I could see only one set of footprints.

So I said to the Lord,
"You promised me Lord,
that if I followed you,
you would walk with me always.
But I have noticed that during
the most trying periods of my life
there have only been one
set of footprints in the sand.
Why, when I needed you most,
have you not been there for me?"

The Lord replied,
"The times when you have
seen only one set of footprints,
is when I carried you."

I found my place in the world. I stand strong, peaceful, secure, and anchored in a deep, loving truth.

Meet the Contributor

CHRISTINE HEART SAVAGE is a teacher, life skills educator, speaker, radio presenter, and stress management and breath awareness expert — she is also known as the "Breathing Lady." Christine is a lively, informative, and fun presenter who has walked the road of anxiety, stress, and breakdown and now lives a life of balance, harmony, and freedom. Since 1994 she has taught people how to desensitize stress responses, correct neural and hormonal patterns, and create a better life for themselves through breath awareness, right thinking, and proper action. She says, "The secret is in the cells" and the breath is the bridge. Her workshops are recommended and described by medical doctors and mental health workers as transformative, profound, and healing.

Contact Christine at www.breatheforlife.com.au

SUCCESS IN REAL ESTATE

John Madden (LBT #67)

IN 2001, I started investing in foreclosure properties. At breakfast with Dave, a realtor friend, I asked him to let me know about any great deals on foreclosures. I had only heard the word "foreclosure" a few times, and wanted to see what one looked like.

He called me a few days later out of breath, and said, "Get over to East Marine View Drive. I'll meet you there."

I arrived first and found a window open, which looked like a fine place to enter the property. A milk crate helped me to get up high enough to jump in and have my first inspection. I couldn't wait to see what this place was all about.

Dave showed up after I'd had the opportunity to check the place out, and I told him to write it up. I would buy it.

I was nervous. I didn't know how much work it was going to be, but wanted to prove to a few people what could be done with a junker property.

The first week was hauling garbage. Four twenty-yard dumpsters later, the yard was cleared, and the rats and dead cats were gone.

Remodeling took place on evenings and weekends for six months, and the house was rented about a week after the finishing touches went on. The people next door were interested, since they had seen every step of the process, and it was nicer than the place they lived in.

They rented the place for two years, and moved out after breaking up. This is where I learned about turnover. One renter after another, the place stayed rented almost solidly, and the damage between them was minimal in most cases.

After getting this first one stabilized, I went after another one, but this time the property was bought to fix and flip. It took three months and about $12,000 for the work; I made $11,000 net on the back end. I was ecstatic.

After buying another three properties to keep, leveraging the first one, I bought another to fix and flip.

THE LESSON

I bought a house outside of our "farm area," which means not understanding the market, and the prices were lower than what I was used to. I failed to negotiate a lower price and used hourly labor, losing $30,000 in the rehab and sale process.

After learning my lesson and licking my wounds, more properties were bought. This time, I went to Kansas City to learn about out of state investing.

Decent houses in fair neighborhoods went for less than $30,000. I fixed them up, and started getting $200 to $300 a month cash flows with each of them. It was well worth having a good property manager to run them, since I couldn't do it alone.

THE DOWNTURN

The rentals were humming along until the market turned down in 2009. Tenants started to make excuses rather than pay rent, or they stayed three months without paying, causing me to evict them. This happened over and over again, until I saw the light.

A friend that worked in the prison system said there were inmates getting out of prison without a place to live or a job; someone with innovative ideas could fulfill those two things. The inmates had support for the first few months they were out, but nobody seemed to be providing long-term services. A few inmates were sex offenders, thieves, and convicted of murder, so they needed special considerations.

I needed a business plan that allowed me to employ these men in such a way they were not a danger to the public. The idea came to me: Why not have them fix and flip our vacant houses? All it took were properties, a plan, and money.

Bank-owned properties were available and I chose carefully. Private money from local investors was used to buy the properties, and the new "residents" did the work. As long as I trained the former inmates, I was eligible for training monies.

All of this new business was fine, but it lacked structure. I trained with a number of real estate gurus, but without solid one-on-one training until I met Loral Langemeier. She said if I didn't have the time or the experience, I needed to buy it. If you need more time, you need more team.

The first thing that came to mind was the financial issue. How could I pay for help if I could barely afford maintenance on the properties?

Looking back over the years I did everything, it became obvious I had done too much of my own work, and spent valuable time doing things I wasn't well suited for. Had I hired help, I could have paid off one holding in full with the savings. I definitely would have enjoyed the process more, and kept a couple of people employed part time as well.

THE BIG DIFFERENCE

THE DIFFERENT REAL estate gurus had great ideas, but never the follow-through offered by Loral's Big Table. It was a nice change to work directly with Loral, not some script-reading technician who represented her.

■ *Meet the Contributor*

JOHN MADDEN IS a real estate investor with over thirty years in the repairs and maintenance business, and a strong professional background in aerospace engineering. His roadblock was fear. Once he developed the tools to manage the fear, he was ready for success. The first deal was nerve-wracking, the second one invigorating, and every one since has been a worthy challenge. He has been engaged in the housing industry for the past eleven years, which allowed him to capitalize on the opportunities in the foreclosure market and the long-term financial security when real estate is bought well and managed right. He has turned one paid-in-full property into nine solid cash-flowing giants. Each property will sprout another junior property in the next five years, and all of them paid off in ten years. Redoubling every five years is the plan going forward, and the sky is no longer the limit.

Contact John at www.readyremodeling.com

Go Where the People Are, Go Where the Money Is

An Artist's Strategy For Offline Marketing

Janet Arline Barker (LBT #63)

When I took the leap from hobby to career artist, part of my passion was to bring art to people who might never attend an art show or enter a gallery.

My first goal was to make a painting a day for two weeks to confirm my passion for painting and create a collection of work. I painted memorable sunsets that shaped my life. To meet this ambitious goal I painted on miniature canvases sized three-by-five and five-by-seven inches. Each sunset consumed me as I relived my experience in those special places. The result was fourteen colorful, inspiring scenes, and great delight in what I had accomplished. Displayed on miniature easels or in small photo frames, they were affordable and small enough to fit almost anywhere in a home or office. Equally delightful, I was able to sell them. Next I made digital images, transferred them to note cards and calendars, and sold them to co-workers, friends, and family during the holiday season.

I live in one of the most scenic areas in the world, practically next door to San Francisco and its urban landscape coupled with views across the bay and out to sea. A two-hour drive takes me south to the coastal regions of Monterey, Carmel, and Big Sur, or north to the delights of the Napa Valley wine country. From all over the world, people travel to Northern California. For some it is a once in a lifetime trip, and for others it is a vacation tradition, a wedding, or the pleasure of having a second home.

If people were drawn to my part of the world because of its beauty, they would enjoy leaving with something representative of that beauty. Why couldn't I provide that? I had the miniatures, note cards, and calendars to add to my collection of framed plein air paintings, altogether a mix of reasonably priced artwork.

■ THE BIRTH OF A BUSINESS

THREE MONTHS AFTER completing the sunset paintings, I took my inventory and visited galleries and gift shops in the regions depicted by my landscapes and seascapes. A number of shops agreed to sell my work on consignment. The sales came. It was a joy to pick up my money and replenish the sold products. After six months I realized my sales, although gratifying, were not going to pay the bills, much less enable me to invest for the passive income I wanted. I wondered how I could take what I knew and loved, and turn it into more cash soon. That's when I decided to sell wholesale with payments due upon delivery. I removed my artwork from stores paying consignment and found new ones to buy wholesale.

Something more had to change, and it was me. I was not acting as a true entrepreneur; I still thought and acted like I had a W-2 job but was on vacation.

To run my business as an entrepreneurial artist I needed in-depth knowledge of all the elements comprising a profitable business. Loral Langemeier's Big Table program and her business and marketing workbooks saved me. To learn more about the art market, I joined three established art associations in different locations, took workshops, networked, and participated in their plein air painting events. I discovered many artists define success as getting juried into prestigious shows, where a sophisticated audience appraised the work; selling was not necessarily the goal. My marketing strategy started to crystallize.

I needed the business to be profitable. I got out of my comfort zone and behaved like an entrepreneur. It was time to end my vacation, build a team, and declare, "I am an artist entrepreneur. I have a business to build."

With this new mindset, I couldn't do everything myself. As cash flow stabilized I added part-time contractors as team members. They included a bookkeeper, copy editor, writer, packaging assistant, and a virtual assistant. Six months later I came to another realization, "I am an idea person." I have the talent and ability to create quality paintings and beautiful photographs, make videos, and write about my feelings and experiences, but my ideas for monetizing these required a team with creative talent. So I searched for creative contractors. My urgency was building a sustainable business. Just staying busy was not the answer. I needed a business plan and marketing strategy. Consequently I focused on offline marketing by making appointments, meeting people face-to-face, and selling in high traffic venues like farmers markets, craft shows, scenic overlooks, and stores where tourists shop.

OFFLINE MARKETING COMES ALIVE

I AM ACTIVE in various community organizations, teach art in an after-school program at the local library, and speak at adult centers. Almost daily I am out in the community and local parks with my canvas, camera, and notepad. Communicating with people of all ages is an absolute delight and a unique chance to engage others in the beauties of the natural world. In addition, my involvement with the chamber of commerce gives me the opportunity to practice the art of selling myself as well as my work.

Developing an offline marketing strategy proved to be very much like the creative process I use in making a painting.

When I choose a subject for artistic expression, I want it to hold my interest and delight others. My business is art, specifically a creative, communicative combination of artwork and written or spoken words.

At first I relate to my subject in a simple, straightforward way. For example, I focus on an elderly oak in a pastoral setting before adding the defining details. I put myself, and my soul, into the work. Finally I draw people into the process and into the finished work.

When I ventured into the world of marketing I had not specifically defined my subject or focus. In nature there was so much to see. My paints and my canvas were prepared, but how to choose? As with setting a goal or choosing a subject to paint, I had to start by getting a better perspective of the outcome I wanted. I had to prepare for marketing just as I prepared to paint. I had to put myself into it; I had to draw others to me, and my work, and excite something in them so they would want to join me.

Once I define the focal point in the painting, I simplify the message into a central theme. In the earlier example, I want people to first look at the heart of the oak tree. The focal point in my offline marketing is to direct customers to artwork representing a place with memories or meaning for them or someone they know.

What makes my business unique? What is specific to this particular oak? I share nature stories that tell life stories through pictures and words, specifically the beauty and wonders of nature. The oak also shares its beauty and the wonder of its structure, limbs twisting with age but outspread with grace, carrying the message of overcoming.

To compose a painting I bring together the details required to communicate a specific message. These details work together to support the main theme or enhance the focal point. Compositional elements are essential to keeping the viewer interested and wanting more. Likewise, successful marketing results in sales because you have captured the customer's attention and held it long enough to create a feeling or thought that encourages them to make a purchase.

The elements to complete a composition include:

* *Organization.* A painting is organized into a foreground, midground, and background. To organize my marketing, I set up easily accessible shelving. Tote bags are packed with supplies for

each of my target regions. In the bags are brochures, samples, and price sheets compatible with my targeted customers. User-friendly pieces enable an efficient sales process.

* *Balance.* A painting is balanced through the strategic placement of various elements in different shapes and sizes. For balanced marketing, I select large businesses with high sales volume and smaller stores in a niche most likely to buy and resell my products. I provide regional art to resort hotels, galleries, tour bus stops, coffee shops, souvenir shops, museum stores, and stores in airports and other transit facilities.

* *Variety.* When painting I work with a variety of colors using various size brushes and apply paint dimensionally, thick and thin, usually in layers. Originally my offerings consisted of canvases and their offshoot products — cards and calendars. I have since developed themed products for specialty shops. An invitation for people to join in the process of painting and the exploration of nature, particularly trees, is also part of my marketing. I achieve this using a varied approach involving published articles and books, public speaking, and workshop events.

Just as painting requires certain tools, my marketing tools start with my totes that are always ready to go, and replenished as necessary. I also have a master list of target customers and businesses, organized by sales regions, and a merchant account to accommodate credit card sales. Although my marketing strategies originated and continue successfully offline, I market myself online too. I have websites for credibility and showcasing my inventory of paintings. I participate in social media and blogging to increase public awareness of what I have to offer and the advantages of inviting nature into everyday life and the artistic process.

Although the process of growing a business is painful at times, I am rewarded with "a-ha" moments. As an example, I had more opportunities to sell my art (as well as be more creative and productive) when I spent time in nature and out talking with people. While selling art at a local farmer's market, I was asked to write a bimonthly art column

for an online newspaper, Patch.com. A month later, two neighboring towns launched their local Patch.com newspapers and I approached the editors for a column with my photos, paintings, and videos about their local trees. Now I am a regular paid columnist for three newspapers, each with unique stories.

The accountability and mastermind calls in the Big Table program include more than just business. They remind me of my successes, that I have a responsibility to share art and the wonders and beauty of nature with others, and they give me the heart and desire to keep going even when I feel stuck.

Once, when my money reserves had dwindled, I found a large and unanticipated check from the sale of my work in my mailbox. I knew then I had to put everything I had, more than just money, into creating a successful business as an artist. I had set my goal, took the correct practical steps, and now I had to recognize and be grateful for my talent and the new opportunities coming to me. Deep down, I know I will achieve my goal, supply is unlimited, and I will have what I need when I need it.

One of the most important things I have learned is that it is impossible to build a long-term business and have multiple streams of income without a team.

▇ THE MAGIC BRUSHSTROKE

THE FINISHING TOUCH is the magic brushstroke. After meeting a new person, potential customer, or as I leave a sales appointment, I say, "Here's something special for you to enjoy." It's what I call a leave-behind-piece. It has value and is an enticement for them to want more of my products and services. Most important, it is memorable and contains my contact information. This leave-behind-piece carries the same spontaneous energy of the magic brushstroke that completed my painting.

I am passionate about sharing the beauties and wonders of nature with others. The natural world has all the answers and inspiration required to live a productive and fulfilling life. My responsibility is to relate these truths to others.

▧ *Meet the Contributor*

JANET ARLINE BARKER's life work has been sharing the wonders and beauties in nature with others. She has taught science and outdoor educational programs in Colorado, Montana, California, and Washington, D.C. Janet used her creative skills in teaching, by combining art with science to enhance observation and learning skills in her students. She also worked eighteen years in the creative arts industry as a graphic designer, illustrator, photographer, and artist. Inspired by nature, she captures the intensity and subtleties of her surroundings. In her words, "The process of plein air painting and nature photography is a peaceful and expressive journey — a dance with brush or camera in hand, propelled by color, infused with fresh air and the sounds of nature." Her published art and nature stories are illustrated with original paintings, photos, and musical video clips. She brings art to people using representations of places that hold inspiration or memories, for area residents and travelers alike.

Contact Janet at www.BarkerInternationalGroup.com

A WOMAN IN A MAN'S WORLD

Lorraine Conaway (LBT #36)

WITH FOURTEEN YEARS of experience in the retail and fashion industry, I made a crazy decision to get into the insurance and financial industry. What was I thinking? I was burned out on the demanding schedule of working weekends, evenings, and holidays.

I graduated from the Fashion Institute of Design and Merchandising at the age of twenty, and had multiple offers with high-end stores to become a buyer for them. The issue for me was that I had to travel to Europe twice a year at minimum, and New York on a regular basis. At such a young age I struggled with the choices because I was getting married and wanted to be with my husband and start a family. If I would have chosen that path I may not be where I am today.

Since I had spent so many years in retail, I thought, "How hard could a financial career be with fourteen years of sales experience?" Boy, was I wrong. I had to learn annuities, stocks, beta factors, and standard deviation, and know what Bull and Bear meant. My head was spinning. I had no experience in the financial world nor had my parents discussed money with me. I told myself to think of key pictures and remember words and meaning when I took the securities exam — which I had to take twice. I have always been a visual learner. To retain the terminology I related it to pictures. One picture was of a bear. They have claws and stand tall and look down, so this became my "down market" symbol. My picture for the up market was represented by the horns on a bull, which pointed upward. This is how I was able to remember and retain details like this in a new industry.

In 1990 at the age of twenty-nine I got my first job in this new career path. I walked into a corporate office where there were only three women and approximately twenty men. On that first day the assistant manager approached me, offering to coach and teach me the business under his wing. Over time we established a great friendship. He invited me to his church, which happened to be the same church I had been attending on a regular basis. This was during a very difficult time when I was getting a divorce and losing my mom and best friend to breast cancer at the young age of fifty-two. I was also raising my two small children, aged two and five, and selling my home for less than I owed in the disintegrating real estate market of the early nineties. I wasn't aware of short sales so I ended up paying for the home I sold over the next ten years on a personal note to the lender to make up the short fall.

Each day was a struggle. I was overwhelmed with all I had to learn, on top of the discrimination of being a woman and of Latin descent. The men ruled and they knew it. It was easier for them to be taken seriously. In order to obtain appointments with new prospects I had to knock on doors of many businesses and repeatedly prove my skills and knowledge. I looked younger than I was and constantly tested with questions to see if I knew what I was talking about.

I had to study twice as hard. I wore glasses so I could look more studious even though I didn't need glasses. One evening I called existing clients of the company to review their investments and obtain an appointment. I called what appeared to be an older man, as his voice was a little shaky and slow paced. It turned out to be his answering machine. He said to leave a message at the tone of the beep. I said "Hello" and stated my name and company, and that the purpose of my call was to discuss his existing A NUDITY contract. Then I exclaimed, "Oh, my God," and hung up in embarrassment. Once again I thought, "What am I doing in this business?"

The company had Monday morning meetings, where the men boasted how well they did the previous week on their sales and production. I couldn't fit the puzzle pieces together on how to increase sales as I was only scheduling ten to fifteen appointments per week. When I asked the men how they were able to close so much business, they replied, "Hard work."

I started taking classes in 1991 through the Councils course in Maryland. These courses were offered in live classrooms in Southern California, which worked out well for me. This is where I established my Life Underwriter Training Council (LUTCF) designation in 1995.

During those years I felt like I was punched in the nose many times. For instance, when I learned exciting concepts about estate planning and wealth accumulation, I spoke about it to new prospects. An older man told me, "Young lady, go back to the drawing board with your information and don't come back." I had stated a fact incorrectly. It was an honest mistake but not tolerated in the financial industry, especially from a thirty-something woman. I sat in my car and cried. What was I doing? I had to perform at 110 percent all the time.

During those years women were a minority and still are today, just at a lower rate. I went back to the office and told my business associate and friend that I wanted out of the business. He said, "No way — you are too good and this industry needs you." I picked myself up and hit the pavement. Once again, I knocked on doors of business owners and shared what I learned from my courses.

In 1993 I married my co-worker and best friend, James O. Conaway. We worked together and built a client base. Over the next three years I felt confident and ready to expand my wings. In 1996 James and I started Conaway & Conaway. We hired an office manager and a part time employee. We were excited about the decision. Not long after our grand opening, James developed diabetes and was rushed to emergency with a blood sugar of 530. At those levels it is common for a person to go into a diabetic coma and die. He could not work for almost three months and I was alone in the new business. I had to let our office manager go.

Once James came back to work we strategized on how to rebuild. Praise God we were able to build the business back quickly. In 1998 we merged with another financial planning firm where we were minority shareowners. That was a fantastic experience. We built a solid firm with over thirty advisors, constructed a commercial building, and had a Cessna airplane. I was the vice president of the firm and our partner was the president and CEO. This lasted for six years. However, like many partnerships we decided to go our separate ways.

Starting again in 2004 as Conaway & Conaway was a new challenge. My husband and I started with one full time employee and one part time person. We moved our office to Orange County, California. During this time the real estate market was booming. I dived into it with a partner who was my ex-husband's wife. She was a realtor so she handled a lot of the transactions and I did the analysis. At our peak we owned nine properties, many of them multi-units. We also did about six flips per year. Things were riding high. Have you ever thought that the money will never stop? I know I did. Then the economy came crashing down. What an emotional and educational experience that was.

In 2007, James and I saw Loral Langemeier on a wealth cruise with Todd Dotson. She introduced herself as a financial strategist. We were very much intrigued as we were financial strategists and didn't have a business model anywhere near what she was accomplishing.

Even though we had implemented many of the strategies and concepts in her Big Table, we took her course so that we could take our business to the next level. I learned how to establish a product funnel, create product, and write a book and a chapter as I am doing right now. We now have newsletters, radio spots, webinars, seminars, and public speaking engagements where we are main stage platform speakers.

Today I have twelve people on payroll and an affiliate office out of Minnesota. Our sales have hit seven figures including the affiliate office. My business model is set up to expand to ten times the current volume. Our firm is currently working on establishing intellectual property rights that allow us to license out our process to other financial advisors.

In addition, I am jumping back into the real estate marketing and looking at flips and buy and hold — this time with a business plan and an exit strategy before starting.

Life is great. I thank my best friend and spouse, James, for being by my side and will always be forever grateful to Loral for her coaching and giving us the opportunity to be vendors at her platform. But the greatest gift I have is my faith in God. Without God nothing is possible.

▪ *Meet the Contributor*

WITH OVER TWENTY years' experience, financial strategist Lorraine Conaway has helped clients nationwide find clarity and confidence in their financial futures. She creates comprehensive financial plans incorporating traditional values with non-traditional strategies for business owners, real estate investors, charities, families, and individuals. She coordinates her efforts with a client's tax advisor, attorney, and other power team professionals to address overall goals while focusing on their risk tolerance and tax needs. Lorraine holds a Certified Retirement Counselor (CRC) and Certified Specialist in Planned Giving (CSPG) designation. Together with her husband and business partner James Conaway they have raised over twenty million dollars in planned gifts for various charities. In April of 2011 Lorraine and James launched their radio show, "Smart Money Talk Radio" on a KNBC affiliate station. Along with the radio she continues to enjoy educating people in various speaking engagements across the country on how to be smart with their money. Lorraine is a registered representative of and offers access to securities through J.P. Turner & Company, LLC (member SIPC). She is an advisory representative of and offers access to investment advice and financial planning through J.P. Turner & Company Capital Management, LLC. J.P. Turner & Company, LLC and J.P. Turner & Company Capital Management, LLC are not affiliated with Conaway & Conaway nor with Loral Langemeier.

Contact Lorraine at www.conawayandconaway.com

SHE INSPIRED ME, THEN BETRAYED ME

Tracie Hammelman

SHE WAS THE type of woman that every woman wished she looked like, and every man wished he could date. She was five-foot nine, dark brown hair, hazel eyes, slim, fine features, and carried herself with grace. She had an IQ that was equally as impressive. She lived to the fullest and challenged herself by living on the edge.

I met Alex when I placed an ad online asking for help with my website. She answered the ad and told me computers were one of her specialties. She gave me some pointers on my website and was on her way.

A couple of years passed, and I started my new business. I created another website and decided to look up Alex. I emailed her, and a couple of weeks later, she responded. She was ecstatic to learn I had written a book and in the process of publishing, and was willing to help with my website.

We met for a drink a few days later, and she revealed that she had developed cancer in her abdomen during the time we lost contact. She completed three rounds of chemotherapy and three rounds of radiation, and planned to start alternative treatment methods beginning the next day. Surgery was not an option because the doctors could not definitively see the entire mass and were afraid of not getting it all, or creating another outlet for the cancer to spread. At this point, her cancer was supposedly contained within scar tissue.

Over the course of a few months, we became fast friends and got together each time she was in town. She told me great stories about her life and kept me updated on her medical treatment, and I told her about the progress on my book. I thought, "This is somebody who really has enriched my life. She is someone who I will keep in touch with no matter where our paths take us."

Her medical situation prompted me to think about my own mortality. I was age forty-eight, and being middle age coupled with the thought anything could take my life tomorrow, made me accelerate my business plan much faster than I would have otherwise. I did not want to be one of those people whose life had passed with nothing to show for it. Worse, I did not want to go to my grave with, as Wayne Dyer said, "my music still in me."

Knowing I had the support of Alex and having a burning desire to tell the world about my book, I scheduled three conferences which I would perform with only two months lead-time. This will really impress Alex, I thought to myself.

In the meantime, Alex and three men formed a security company like KBR. She mentioned she used some of her own money to invest in the company and getting great returns on her investment. I knew the cost of the conferences were going to be high and the thought of making an investment that would cover my costs was irresistible.

I gave her the money, we devised and signed a contract, and she told me I would get fifty percent on my money after one month, one hundred percent return after two months, and 200 percent return after four months.

The conference dates were fast approaching, and thoughts of my investment took a back burner. I am the type of person to accomplish goals once I make up my mind, and these events were no exception. However, I was on a collision course with one of the biggest fears in my life: public speaking. My emotions reached new highs as I mailed out the 11,000 conference flyers to licensed psychotherapists in Houston, Dallas, and San Antonio. A little voice in my head asked, What if they all show up?

I developed hives all over my body and they remained until the conferences were over. I took Benedryl and applied cortisone cream, but nothing helped. The itching was out of control, and I scratched my skin raw in some areas. I also could not sleep, or when I did, it was not restful.

My anxiety about doing this event was so high I thought I was having a heart attack. In fact, it was only a panic attack, but still scary. My doubts grew out of control: What if they don't like me, what if they reject me, what if they heckle me, what if I freeze up on stage? What if I can't write a speech that is entertaining, educational, and inspirational? What if I don't have an answer to a question, will they think that I am stupid or a fool for trying to do such an endeavor?

There were times prior to the conference dates when I would ask myself if I was crazy to take on such a seemingly insurmountable task. The good thing was I had already signed contracts with the hotels and sent out the flyers so I could not back out of the deal.

For the content for the conference, I finished the PowerPoint slides at five in the afternoon the day before the conference, left Houston, drove five hours to Dallas, and tried to sleep. I slept until two in the morning, then another idea popped into my head, and I got up and added another slide to my presentation. The topic of my book focused on integrating psychotherapy with quantum physics and the Laws of Attraction, and the conference purpose was to introduce attendees to these concepts and teach how to apply them.

To my surprise, the persistence paid off. I became an approved Continuing Education Unit (CEU) provider for the state of Texas and delivered the conferences with great success. The experience of being in the zone, doing what I love to do, and getting glowing reviews was worth the strife I went through.

But I still had much to learn. I gave money to Alex as an investment to help cover the cost of conducting the conferences. After the conferences were over, I asked Alex about the money. She gave me answers that seemed legitimate and I allowed time to pass. I continued with this for six months and I saw no money. Ignoring the warning signs, I sent her the raw video footage from the conferences (DVD production and editing were among the many skills she claimed to have).

Alex told me she completed the editing at the end of September, but she never returned the DVDs or investment to me. I filed a lawsuit against her and she could not be served because she had moved to Fort Worth. To add insult to injury, I dedicated my book to her and could not withdraw it because the book had been printed.

As entrepreneurs, you will encounter challenges not unlike the ones I have described. Here are my recommendations on how to overcome these obstacles:

1. When doubt and fear set in, remain focused on your goals and be persistent in achieving them — success comes to those who do not give up.

2. When presented with an investment opportunity, no matter how big or small, have respect for your money and perform extensive due diligence before making the decision to invest.

3. When planning your own events, plan them with a revenue model that makes them economically sustainable on their own (versus relying on an investment for funding).

The one thing of comfort is learning about quantum physics and the Laws of Attraction. It is a common belief with heart-centered entrepreneurs, that if you tithe, you get a return that is at least three times the amount that you gave. Along those same lines, it is also a belief that if you fail to pay your bills or fulfill your contracts or obligations with people, that financial hardship will come back to you also at least threefold. I have chosen to let go of the situation with Alex, and allow the universe to handle it for me.

Meet the Contributor

Tracie L. Hammelman, LCSW, is known as "The Advocate for Mental Health Professionals" and "has put quantum physics and the law of attraction on the mental health map." Tracie is the author of *Psychotherapy for the 21st Century: Quantum Physics and The Law of Attraction*. The book is the first of its kind in the psychotherapy industry, and according to her brother (who is not biased), she has been a trendsetter for many years. She leads a Quantum Mentoring Program designed to help other psychotherapists build their businesses. She has practiced psychotherapy for over twenty years and owns 21st Century Holistic Health, LLC, in Houston, Texas. She received her bachelor of business administration degree from the University of Iowa in 1983 and master of social work degree from the University of Iowa in 1990. She retired as a major in the Air Force Reserves after twenty-six years of honorable service in March 2010. Contact Tracie at www.21stcenturypsychotherapy.com

Is Your Business
Suffering Anorexia?

Nancy Hopkin (LBT #74)

ALL I WANTED to do was to be a mother with children who loved God, each other, and me. As a young mother I was told, "You have the perfect *Leave it to Beaver* family."

I was taken aback and thought, That's because you don't know what goes on when you're not here.

We looked like the perfect family: my husband was a physician and I was a stay-at-home mom raising six beautiful children. Wherever we went, we sang in harmony: at community functions and church, and in public transportation. Although we had a television for movies, we didn't watch network programming in our home. We had family scripture study and family prayer each day in addition to a family hour each week. We didn't watch R-rated movies. The kids were 4.0 students — involved in school and church with many extra-curricular activities. We didn't have junk food in our home. We ate dinner as a family, often waiting until eight o'clock for my husband to come home from work. I volunteered many hours at school and church. We sent three children to college on scholarships for talent and academics.

But something was not right. One early morning, I had a call from my daughter, Hannah. "Mom," she said sobbing, "I am so unhappy. I don't know what is wrong." We'd had several talks about her recent weight loss, and she agreed to make an appointment with a counselor in town. He told me to relax and he would let me know when I should start worrying. Unable to do anything else, I followed his orders.

Months later he called me. "Are you worried yet?"

I said, "I'm waiting for you to tell me when I should be." With much work behind-the-scenes, we convinced Hannah to agree to go to the Center for Change in Orem, Utah — a live-in facility for eating disorders. At five-five and weighing seventy-six pounds, she had a full-blown case of anorexia nervosa. Karen Carpenter had it and she died. I couldn't allow that to happen. Yet, Hannah's illness was particularly strong.

Serious addiction (for which anorexia has definite earmarks) is an indicator that the family is in trouble. Similar symptoms of illness can be found in many businesses. Anorexia is not an individual issue, but a family issue. At least one parent must act or change, or the family will continue in a downward spiral. Just like any business owner experiencing marketing, sales, leadership, or personnel problems, everyone is involved and affected. I had a choice to make: pay the personal price necessary to help all of us get well or pretend it was out of my hands. Many business owners are faced with similar choices.

It was past time to be accountable. I needed to change some behaviors. It would be much more difficult for my children to recover if I allowed our family to remain as they were. I wanted to fight for our wellbeing and chose to act upon these discoveries. I simplified my schedule, dropped what I was doing when someone wanted to talk, listened and cried a lot, stopped blaming my husband, trusted principles more than feared outcomes, let go of my pride, and went in search of my lost laughter.

And it worked. Hannah is eight years out of the Center and thriving. She graduated in April 2011 with a master of social work degree, and intends on working with other women who have this potentially fatal disease. All my children have made significant course-corrections and continue to work hard for peace in their soul. Every human being needs to know their parents love them regardless of their decision of how to live their life.

Hannah's illness, although fraught with turbulence and darkness, offered tools for my life. I had no idea whether death or I would win, but I was determined to learn and change. For a long time, I felt like a failure. However, as I have seen my children work hard to overcome their weaknesses over the years, I have also seen them drawing closer to God, each other, and to me. As each one grows in confidence, clarity of purpose, and ability to dream, I realize I did a lot of things well.

The same power tools that allowed my children and I to survive this crisis apply to entrepreneurs in almost any stage of their business. Now is the time for you to be honest with yourself about your business. Below are the five power tools that enabled me to successfully raise my children in the middle of our crisis, and I explain how they apply to you and your business.

1. Do you promise to deliver more things than is possible without help? Hannah could have never recovered her health without a support team. Although we, her family, were the most important members of her support team, we were no good to her without the help from medical doctors, dieticians, psychologists, family therapists, art therapists, dance therapists, recreational therapists, researchers, music therapists, and the other patients residing at the Center. Each had their own area of expertise, making their part of the prescription perfect. Doing everything yourself works against your goal. Not only do you slow down the production process but you also lose awareness of your possibilities. It is more fun to work with other people, as it decreases stress, increases creativity and productivity, provides more jobs, better quality, and strengthens the economy. Who could ask for more?

2. Do you ask your employees or clients their opinion when you are about to launch a new product or service? Before I sought counseling I put everything I knew into being a good mother. I dropped what I was doing to take the forgotten lunch to school, fix the hair, listen to the broken heart, and help with the homework, "knowing" that it was the best any child could hope for. It never occurred to me that the mental and emotional gymnastics needed to make those things possible had created such stress. I was giving something that my children did not need. They tried to tell me,

but I did not listen. In the business world, like life at home, every effort matters. If you want to launch a new product or service, always ask those in your niche market about their needs and be clear with your question. Consider whom you are trying to serve, your ego or your customers?

3. Are you aware of your employees' strengths and weaknesses and do you leverage their strengths where possible? It never occurred to me that each child had a different learning style. With that small difference came a different sense of time, a different interest in various things, and a different approach to life. Nor did I consider that my to-do list around the house was a service to my children. How much more enjoyable would life have been if I had given them a list of options for their Saturday chores? You cannot always let your employees choose their work assignments, but honoring each applicant's differences and strengths can help you get the right person for the job. If you have a clear job description when you set out to hire someone, you will design better questions to help you determine how profitable the proposed joint venture will be. Keep in mind that your job-offer is a blessing to someone; you will be better able to serve each other.

4. Are you aware of your emotions? More importantly, are you able to work them out so they aren't worked out on your employees? Because I was afraid to make some crucial decisions about my marriage, I decided to "fake it until we made it." Unfortunately, leaving basic things unattended leads to emotional decay on the whole family or business. It doesn't take long before the whole company is running on numb energy. Trust that you have control over your personal life, and never get to a point where people become insecure about how you are going to respond to a given situation. You need them to talk to you as much as they need you to lead the company. You must never minimize the effect of your positive leadership.

5. When was the last time you expressed gratitude for a job well done? By the time Hannah was showing her illness, I was immersed in

my own state of un-wellness. We both needed praise and acknowledgement and neither of us were getting or giving it enough to those around us. I determined to offer prayers of thanksgiving each night when I went to bed. There were nights when I had to think harder than others, but the effort began to spill over into the daytime interactions with other members of my family. The edges of our hearts began to soften. Think of gratitude as light in an otherwise dark place. Don't we all work better in the light?

In closing, I leave you with a most fascinating and fathomable challenge: if the life you are wearing is uncomfortable, it is time to clean out the closet and get a new wardrobe.

▓ *Meet the Contributor*

When Nancy Hopkin began directing a children's choir at church when twelve years old, she had no idea what kind of power and influence music would have on her own life. Since then she has inspired thousands of students to higher spiritual and emotional ground through her work. She has taught many choirs for children, boys, girls, and adults. Most recently, she directed a women's choir and several musicianship courses at Brigham Young University–Idaho. She loves working with students, and they love her. Nancy is the mother of six grown children and the grandmother of three. After becoming part of the team that helped her daughter not only survive but thrive after an eating disorder, she became passionate about increasing public awareness and teaching others how to cope with and support loved ones who have an eating disorder. Constantly amazed with the number of people around her who are suffering with the disease, she strives to help others embrace who they truly are without fear, develop healthy boundaries, cope with external expectations, and get past their own history. Contact Nancy at www.EatingDisordersHelp.com

THE FIFTY-YEAR-OLD ORPHAN

LIFE AFTER CORPORATE AMERICA

Vanessa Jackson (LBT #72)

WHILE MANY DOWNSIZED professionals see themselves as corporate America casualties, I was more like a fifty-year-old orphan. For thirty years it had been a nurturing and generous parent. I felt abandoned because unlike many others, I was not yet burned out. Quite the opposite, I was a favored child.

My corporate career was full of accomplishment and achievement for which I had been generously rewarded. There were promotions, bonuses, and even a three-year international assignment. A large part of my good fortune was due to timing. I came out of college with a master's degree in marketing during the time when an MBA was a golden passport to corporate management. Some of my success can be attributed to my devotion, loyalty, and love for what I did. I once said that if I won the lottery, I wouldn't quit my day job. I'd be more selective in the assignments I took on, but what else would I do with my time?

Departure from the company that downsized me was not traumatic because I had already decided to leave. But in no way was I prepared for what followed.

I approached the job search enthusiastically and with the same tenacity I'd applied to other challenges in my career. Spreadsheets with lists of local companies cluttered my home office. I designed introduction cards and mailed them to a couple hundred human resource and marketing contacts on my target company list. I joined every professional organization and attended networking events ad nauseam. I was certain a new corporate opportunity lay just around the corner.

◼ A Crushing Realization

Optimism became frustration. I was not accustomed to hearing the word "no." After more rejections than I care to remember, something hit me: I was fifty years old and maybe that affected my lack of success. Much like the adolescent orphan, my future was more uncertain than I thought. The realization was devastating. I felt betrayed. It wasn't just business, it was personal. My identity had been tied to my career for so long. I was a first generation college graduate and successful professional. I was the pride of my family and the envy of my friends.

When you pray for strength, what you get is not strength but a situation that demands you are strong. This was more than a career crisis; it was a life crisis, and a journey that had already begun.

◼ The Writing on the Cubicle Wall

People have a remarkable capacity to see only what they want to see. By every measure I considered myself content. I was hardworking, often exhausted, but satisfied with my place in the world.

As day-to-day life became quieter, something new broke through. How could I have missed it? I thought of myself as the well put-together professional but my life was more fragile than I acknowledged. I was held together by the antidepressants I'd taken for several years, and a stay in a rehabilitation center several years earlier was for more than exhaustion. I felt like a marionette that had become aware of her strings.

▨ MAKING A NEW LIFE

I HAD TO pick up the pieces of a life too long ignored. My career had been a convenient distraction from many things that were crumbling around me. Some of the broken pieces were small, and some were big. One was enormous — the relationship with my thirteen-year-old daughter.

At the time of the downsizing, my daughter was living with her father, my ex-husband, in California. I couldn't handle the rebellious attitude that came with adolescence. I was far too busy with work to work on our relationship. Before I knew it, the distance between us was too wide for me, the superwoman, to leap in a single bound. Instead of trying, I took the advice of a family therapist (yes, it had gotten that bad) and sent her to live with her father.

Moments of clarity are different for everyone. Some describe them as their "a-ha" moment and others speak of a sudden revelation. When the moment came for me, I exhaled. How long had I been holding my breath? Years of disillusion vaporized to reveal a disturbing truth. I'd made a great living at the expense of having a great life.

I knew what I wanted to do, no matter how impossible it seemed. I wanted to be a better mother to my only child. I needed to stay home with my daughter for the next three years until she graduated. After years of devotion to my career, the idea of being a single stay-at-home mom seemed preposterous.

▨ THE RELUCTANT ENTREPRENEUR

BECOMING AN ENTREPRENEUR was a necessity borne from the new path I'd chosen. I was unprepared in every way, but determined. Corporate America had prepared me for many things; flying solo was not one of them.

Eighteen months later, after a disastrous foray into real estate followed by a half-hearted effort to build a home travel business, I felt like I was trying to push a string. Frustrated and out of ideas, I ran across the following words that resonated deep within me:

To achieve something that you have never achieved before,
you must become something that you have never been before.
— Les Brown

That was what I needed. With renewed energy, I set out to learn about being an entrepreneur.

"When the student is ready, the teacher appears," says the Zen proverb. A friend invited me to a three-day Cash Machine workshop. I'd never heard of Loral Langemeier, and there I sat in a room surrounded by others who were doing what I wanted to do. Over those three days I listened to different stories of how each came to be there. For some, being an entrepreneur was a life long intent while for others, it was an escape from the stifling corporate bureaucracy. For the first time, I respected and appreciated my own story.

Loral's philosophy is simple but brilliant. Uncover the skills you have, come up with a moneymaking idea around those skills, test the idea to make sure you can make money quickly, then execute and perfect the idea later.

This helped me focus my energy. I realized what I had been doing wrong. None of the previous endeavors leveraged my strengths. I was a thirty-year marketing professional who had invested years in education and more years of sweat and tears perfecting my craft. I was an acknowledged expert in the specialized marketing field of consumer behavior and brand building. I had worked with the best marketing practitioners in corporate America. It was what I loved to do, so I decided to build my business with this as the core.

One of the principles Loral taught was the sales funnel. Digital content is typically at the top of the funnel while the real cash earner (like paid workshops) is at the bottom. The point is to build relationships with customers at the top and carry them progressively down the funnel.

As I wrote my first book, *Prospect Smarter, Not Harder: The Art and Science of Getting More Customers,* I knew I was in my element. The positive and instructive feedback I received from my book coach, weekly mastermind group, and Live Out Loud community kept me energized.

There was nothing as special as having the first copies of my book sold. One book will never make me wealthy but knowing I could generate any income from my own efforts was priceless. More importantly, my daughter goes to college this fall and there is nothing I would have traded for these past three years.

It's clear to me now. I had not been orphaned but nudged to the edge, and then pushed from the nest so I could learn to fly.

▨ Vanessa's Tips for the Want-to-be Entrepreneur

1. Commit to live in full awareness at all time. Nothing can be successful until you do.

2. Joe Girard said: "The elevator to success is broken. Take the stairs." You may take the scenic route but sometimes the value is in taking the journey, not reaching the destination. Enjoy the view. Learn to honor the process.

3. Build your business around something you love to do. Work and fun are not opposite states of being. Today I find myself giddy for no reason. This is a feeling I assumed was captive to a distant past.

4. Success and wealth have different meanings for each of us. Get clear about what they mean to you.

▨ *Meet the Contributor*

VANESSA BESTEDA JACKSON is a seasoned marketing professional who specializes in consumer behavior marketing. She has held a number of senior positions with several Fortune 500 companies, including Kraft General Foods, SBC Communications, Navistar, and a three-year relocation assignment with Kraft Canada in Montreal, Quebec.

Vanessa earned her BS and MA degrees from Ohio State University in Columbus, Ohio where she grew up. She expects to soon complete an MBA in sustainable development management. She is a speaker, consultant, adjunct marketing instructor, and author of *Prospect Smarter, Not Harder: The Art and Science of Getting More Customers* and numerous marketing articles. She currently lives in Oak Park, Illinois with her seventeen-year-old daughter, Brittany.

Contact Vanessa at vanessa@prospectsmarter.net

THE SABOTEUR

THE MOST POWERFUL OF THIEVES

Jeannette McCarroll (LBT #75)

In 1998, I stepped away from an executive director position of a small non-profit organization and into entrepreneurship. It was frightening and exciting. However, I knew it was time and learned it was right for me.

I capitalized on one of Loral's principles to fast cash: do what you already know how to do. I am organized, fiscally detailed and responsible, love public speaking and marketing, and have the highest integrity. I am the perfect program manager.

I had recently learned to facilitate workshops on positive parenting. As soon as I became self-employed, two non-profit entities approached me to run their state-funded parent education programs. Providence met my commitment to be self-employed by providing these opportunities. In the first year, my salary grew fifty percent from my executive director position and continued to rise.

My contract with the larger of the two programs was extended for a second year and its budget grew, and the program and my salary also grew. I created privately funded opportunities facilitating workshops for the public. Then I was awarded a contract to facilitate effective communication with the local county superior court staff, as well as troubled parents served by the county's behavioral health department. This led to a contract with a local artist designing brochures to help the public understand the different court processes of the municipal and superior courts. Next I worked with federally funded youth programs facilitating workshops in effective communication.

I instinctively knew to first meet with my clients or parents, ask them what they needed, and listen to them. The information was used to design my training programs. As a result, the programs were a huge success with an increasing numbers of participants.

Success was easy when I spent my time doing what I already knew how to do in different environments with diverse populations. Meanwhile, my income continued to increase. The fun and challenging part was repurposing the core principles of my content to serve the different populations.

You're probably thinking, "After thirteen years, she must be a very successful entrepreneur. Maybe she's financially independent and doesn't need to generate an income." Shortly after the pinnacle of that phase in my entrepreneurship, I lost forward momentum and focus. Nonprofit funds were predicted to dry up and instead of repurposing my content to reach greater markets I succumbed to the saboteur.

The saboteur lies in waiting. It is insidious and domineering. It undermines your forward motion, discredits your accomplishments, and negates your success. The saboteur is the judge who whispers the words that mold one's life. It finds fault when things are going well or waits until you are down and then drags you under.

The saboteur was my negative self-image and critic. It dictated the words I used and the actions I took or did not take to create a self-fulfilling prophecy. The saboteur has rigid thinking, which closed doors and robbed me of opportunities. Some examples of my saboteur's language include:

+ I'll never get ahead.

+ I (we) can't afford that.

+ I only need to work hard to make enough money.

◆ I know I will be in debt for the rest of my life and will have to work until I die.

Are these expressions familiar? I said them over and over and I was living them. I was charmed by my saboteur and did not know she existed. It takes special ears to hear the saboteur.

The saboteur ruled my life by keeping me in cyclical thinking. I was attracted to drama and would embellish it. The saboteur found comfort in mulling over the same story. Each time I cycled through the story, I became more entrenched and lost the precious here and now and perpetuated the negative drama of the past. This is the land of the saboteur, the delusion of a negative event relived over and over, robbing me of today and setting up more negativity tomorrow.

The effect of the saboteur was devastating. She convinced me the only way to get ahead was to apply for student loans and go back to school. She said I was not good enough and would not be worthy of more until I became more. I was accepted to a technical college in southern Oregon and found the inner strength and forward action I was used to exercising as an entrepreneur was not acceptable in this environment. I was astonished at how the students were treated and this was an unhealthy environment for me. Still not believing I had the ability to create a better life elsewhere, I left southern Oregon and enrolled in a master of science program, was accepted and applied for more student loans. This program stretched me more than I had ever experienced. Every day I struggled with the saboteur's self-defeating thoughts that I would never make it even though I had good grades. Her influence was relentless and she was never satisfied.

The saboteur took me on a ten-year distraction away from who I really am. She helped me create intense chaos, drama, and paralysis in my life. She persuaded me that others know best when I should work, how I should work, and how much am I worth. The saboteur feeds on negativity and fear.

Several months ago I read three of Loral's books, in addition to works by Napoleon Hill and Claude Bristol, and participated in Loral's CD/workbook sets. Completing the "Expression of Your Power" series dislodged some of the old patterns and mindset of my self-worth. It revealed how I went numb when having conversations around money. It made me aware of inherited deficit thinking and how I wasted time, energy, and resources getting caught up in the drama of others. This distraction took me down nonproductive paths. The coursework gave me the ears to hear my saboteur.

Since I committed to self-exploration and self-improvement, I own that I am entitled to prosperity and abundance, great health, great wealth, harmony, joy, and happiness. This is my commitment to myself. These are mine and I claim them.

I also reclaim my entrepreneurship. It has been and will always be who I am. Today I walk into this part of myself. It is evident by how I present myself to others. It keeps my thoughts open and expansive, and my world is open and expansive.

Being self-employed utilizes all my skills and talents, which makes my life full and rewarding and allows me to serve more people. Being an entrepreneur allows me to follow my own biorhythms and soar when I am moved and regroup when I need. Being an entrepreneur inspires and exhilarates me rather than leaving me exhausted at the end of the day.

Money flows easily into and through my hands. I hire teams of people to support me as I share my knowledge with others. I have the energy and enthusiasm to produce because I am optimistic and inspired when I tap into the good of me. I am my own cheerleader.

What lessons have I learned on this long arduous journey?

- I never lost the entrepreneur in me. She has only been dormant while I was under the spell of the saboteur.

- The spell of the saboteur is pervasive and requires vigilant monitoring as the threads she uses to weave her web are teased out. The longer I listen to her, the less I walk into my power as a human being.

- More importantly, I learned I have a powerful aspect that is the antidote to the saboteur. It is artful at monitoring my thoughts, actions, and words. It chooses the positive words to paint the picture of what my life is and what it will become. It is the good and nonjudgmental me.

I live in abundance and continue to do so by sharing my gifts and talents with people and surround myself with a team to support me on this journey. I do not have to do it all and I will be more successful if I do not. That work is for others, who do it well. My job is to concentrate on the things only I can do. I love this concept because it creates opportunities for all people to shine, which means we share the wealth.

Meet the Contributor

JEANNETTE MCCARROLL IS an entrepreneur and pathologists' assistant. She has a bachelor of science in social sciences, with a depth in family relations, and a master's of science degree as a pathologists' assistant. She is also a certified Life Mastery Consultant specializing in teaching time-proven techniques used to overcome the inner saboteur, thus reducing life's struggle and creating a free flowing path to one's dreams. Contact Jeannette at www. bridgetoyourdreams.com

Viva Lake Las Vegas

Don Saunders (LBT #74)

You, and only you, can take your business to success. Don't look up in the sky or sit on the couch hoping it happens. Don't look for help from your friends, family, or neighbors. They can support, teach, and inspire, but it is up to you and only you.

Every contributor in this book has met obstacles along the way to success. If you were to put all of them in one room, you would notice their common traits: tenacity, confidence, inner strength, focus, pride, spirit, soul, and a sincere interest in the success of the people around them. Many entrepreneurs went on to build mega-companies because they knew the secret business formula and implemented the traits above to build their success.

The subtitle of this book — *How Common People Achieve Uncommon Results* — has defined my life. My wife, Karen, and I are common people that made up our minds to survive a tough economy. We live in the Village at Lake Las Vegas, Nevada. It is truly one of the wonders of the world: a lake in the middle of the desert with restaurants, shops, hotels, and golf. The man that built it was the quintessential entrepreneur. He had a vision (a lake in the middle of a desert); he had a dream (a Tuscan village in the middle of America); and he must have had a few dry martinis to assist him in envisioning people coming to visit and eventually living there. What's not to love about a vision like that? I loved the vision so much I decided Karen and I should relocate from

Dana Point, California overlooking the ocean and harbor to the oasis in the desert referred to as Lake Las Vegas. Please do not ask Karen her opinion on the move — I am still working on convincing her it was a smart thing to do.

At the time it seemed like a tremendous plan. I worked in a W-2 job as vice president of sales in the western area for a big company that I had been associated with for over thirty-five years. Karen landed a job at the Ritz Carlton Resort at Lake Las Vegas. We found a building lot overlooking the golf course and built a home. I joined two championship golf courses and the Village nestled in the resort within a mile of the house had restaurants, shops, and a lake, and since it is Las Vegas, we had a casino within walking distance. For two country kids who grew up in the same rural town in western New York some thirty-five years earlier, we were doing very well. I had prepared for my freedom day.

Freedom day, as Loral Langemeier puts it, is not traditional retirement. This is the day when you have the financial means to live the way you have always wanted, free from financial worries and obligations. Most importantly, it allows you to give back by changing the way the people around the world see Americans and usher in a new era where we care about all humanity and not just ourselves.

You may consider freedom day as the day when you shed your W-2 job and start pursuing those entrepreneurial quests you have always harbored. The fun part is that only you define your freedom day. If you want to play golf, go play golf. If you want to build a business while having fun doing it, there is plenty of help to get you there and you already have accumulated life experiences to call on. If you choose to make millions of dollars so you can help those that have not figured out how to help themselves, follow your dreams and utilize the Laws of the Universe that are available to you. Choose a positive path and be tenacious in your resolve. If you do that without restrictions, I make the following promise: When your intentions are converted from ego-, greed-, and profit-based objectives to positive intentions of helping others, the universe will guide your path and open the doors you believed were closed in the past. Nothing is impossible unless you believe it is.

As an entrepreneur, you can apply the Laws of Attraction (or however you refer to it) and with total confidence build your business and personal life to be extraordinary.

■ THE CRASH

TWO YEARS AFTER moving into the Village at Lake Las Vegas, my freedom day appeared to be doomsday. At least that is how it felt to Karen and I. The company I worked at for thirty-five years sold the division I was part of since the age of nineteen. Because I had not yet hit fifty-five, I lost a significant portion of my retirement annuity and all my earned benefits. The stock market crashed and took what little I had left in the 401K. The economic downturn caused the golf courses to go into bankruptcy, the Ritz Carlton closed, and the casino went out of business. My house value turned upside down and inside out. In addition to the economic issues, I was unhappy in my W-2 job. Depression set in. My business life was a mess.

What does this have to do with being an entrepreneur? Prior to the crash Karen and I decided we better do something to prepare for the day when my W-2 job went away. We chose to follow her passion of having her own southwest jewelry retail business. She left the Ritz Carlton and became an entrepreneur in the Village at Lake Las Vegas. To add to the confusion, we had an opportunity to open two additional galleries. This was a bold move, but we were in the entrepreneurial mode. We opened a Murano glass gallery and a fine art gallery before the businesses (the Ritz and the casino) who would be our customers began closing their doors. People were out of work by the thousands in the surrounding community as the economic downturn hit Las Vegas. Housing values plummeted and there was no expendable cash to buy jewelry, glass, or art. The obstacles were formidable.

We were not in this alone. Merchant friends in the Village were struggling, restaurants in trouble, and neighbors losing their houses. When people look at the Lake Las Vegas lifestyle, on the surface there is not much sympathy for the people like us that bought into the resort. Some people referred to the residents as decadent, but we were ordinary people that worked hard, never hurt anyone on the way up, and felt like we had earned what we bought. Still, it was collapsing around us. I know why it did and what I had to do to survive.

After a couple of very long years in a tough economy, Lake Las Vegas is coming back to life. If you want an example of a business plan gone wrong, a turnaround on the horizon, and the power of positive thinking by entrepreneurs throughout the village, come to Lake Las Vegas and do a case study. Most individuals gave up and let the bad days overcome them, but the people of the Village at Lake Las Vegas have persevered through the hard times. The Village management stepped up to help with the rents where they could. In addition, the shop owners tightened their belts with good management practices such as working the shops as employee/owners, adjusting hours as needed, and working twelve to fourteen hour days instead of playing golf and paying help. We also preserved cash by keeping expenses and inventory purchases to a minimum. Most importantly, we stayed positive through devastating times.

If two country kids from a small town can make it, so can you. Viva Lake Las Vegas.

Meet the Contributor

DON SAUNDERS IS an author, speaker, and entrepreneur. He retired after thirty-eight years in corporate America, where his career culminated with his position as vice president of sales for the western area of a major corporation. He then opened multiple retail establishments. His unique perspectives on today's business environment provide an interesting look into the do's and don'ts of running and managing multiple businesses and motivating people to contribute to a company's overall success. Don applies his knowledge to helping people from all backgrounds and traditional beliefs improve how they approach success and life. His ability to transfer this knowledge in its pure form is what makes it valuable. Contact Don at www.thepowerofknowinghowlifeworks.com

Record-Breaking Results In Half the Time

Tapping into Source Energy

Tracey Thomson (LBT #74)

Before I embarked on creating Integrity Cosmetics, a line of Australian-made, certified organic skin care, I was clear about several things, and the most important was my desire to make a difference on a large scale. I had known this for years and searched for an opportunity that ticked all the boxes.

Being passionate about health and wellbeing, the environment, and philanthropy, I wanted my life's work to have a positive impact and raise the level of consciousness in these areas throughout the world. In my eyes this would benefit all beings, now and in the future. Creating Integrity Cosmetics was a journey I was meant to take. I did not, however, have some of the fundamental knowledge and skills required to succeed. For example, I had no chemistry experience or consumer goods packaging experience, and both are critical for a cosmetics company. To most, this key issue would prevent them from starting. But I was determined to succeed.

The challenge I faced when I created my team was that the key members thought my plan was ambitious and told me I was more or less crazy. To create, produce, and launch a range of certified organic skin care products to market in twelve months wasn't possible. They hadn't seen a project of this type and scale be done in less than three years — the industry average — and some had taken as long as five years. We achieved our goal in eighteen months.

I used unconventional methods to select my team members, create the brand and the products, and launch the company. My team members were all experts in their fields.

How do you embark on such a project without the required knowledge and produce record-breaking results? Most people would say it's easy: just throw more money at it. I did the opposite and achieved my goal with a conservative budget that was self funded, allowing me to retain one hundred percent ownership, and produce the results in half the time my team thought was possible.

Whether at the start of your new venture or part way through, lack of time and or money is a familiar problem for business people. In fact, many entrepreneurs starting new companies and projects never see their dreams fulfilled because they give up after hitting their first brick wall.

I embarked on this venture doing the critical tasks that enabled me to deliver a breakthrough result and launch in less than eighteen months, and with half the budget I had originally forecast was required. (We would have launched in twelve months if not for an issue at the production plant that caused a six-month delay.)

My first task was to secure a business coach. Not just any coach, a coach experienced in tapping into source energy. This proved critical in producing the breakthrough results. I spent three months writing my business plan until my coach and I were happy I had a concise vision and plan. I created the branding brief and everything else followed.

My team commented on how clear my briefs were and how quickly I made decisions and turned tasks around. This was not always my strength, but for this project I was on rails and moving forward and fast.

I was surprised at how little dialogue I had with the chemist during the formulation stage. I provided her with a six-page brief for each product, according to the required format, and I trusted her. I let her be the expert and let her do her job. By empowering her, much time was saved.

The key to concise briefs and fast decision-making was in preparation and process. A critical part of the process included kinesiology and energetic testing. While the formulas had to go through the required biology tests and organic certification requirements, I also did my own testing on the formulas and other areas of the business.

Kinesiology is used by naturopaths and dentists and is a profession in its own right. Kinesiology helps people diagnose health issues and remove blockages in challenging areas of life. I experienced kinesiology when I was in my late twenties and it transformed my health. Several years later, I read a book by Dr. David R. Hawkins that outlined a scale when using kinesiology from zero to 1,000, where 1,000 represented the highest vibration or calibration possible on earth: enlightenment. I had never seen kinesiology or other forms of energetic testing used to create a company, set up a business, produce a new product, or take that product line to market. I wanted to be the first to do this, and I knew it would benefit others.

Tapping into source energy proved to be invaluable. You need to work with experienced practitioners to be assured of accurate results. Moreover, you cannot ask loaded questions (or questions which have no integrity) during kinesiology testing, because the source energy knows and when you tap into source energy it is never wrong. However, you do need to be clear and careful about the questions you ask so that they are not vague, otherwise the results will be of no use. Yes/no questions are ideal. Alternatively, calibrating on a scale from zero to 1,000 also gives you the level of calibration or vibration.

We used kinesiology in scenarios that involved pilot testing, trials, consumer research, my own intuition, and numerous business decisions. This took minutes compared to the usual days or weeks to complete these tasks. When I didn't have access to a practitioner to do testing I did energy tests using a crystal to determine answers.

Then I trusted what I got. This step is important. If you ask source energy for answers and don't follow them, this is a recipe for disaster. Sometimes the results are not what we expect and we don't understand why. This is because there is information we are unaware of and our logical minds do not comprehend the answer. But if you trust, you see why the answer was as it was. We saved months, if not years, of time and thousands of dollars by incorporating kinesiology and energy testing into a sound business plan and project management approach.

The day before my wedding I received a phone call to say that our formulas were approved and had received organic certification. Our packaging could go into production and we were less than three months away from having a product ready to sell. But this was not meant to be and we had a six-month delay. Only when the product was delivered did I know we had done it. I saw the delivery sitting on pallets, all boxed up. We had our marketing collateral and it was time to take our Australian-made certified organic skin care, produced with a difference, to the world.

This was a very unusual approach to business. But I had been involved in cutting edge technologies in the information technology and telecommunications industries, and in the personal development industry. I believed the groundbreaking thinking and approaches we used would lead to extraordinary results. This kept me motivated during the tough times.

If you embark on something different or new you will get people who knock you, question you, doubt you, be jealous, or warn you not to proceed — even when they love you and have your best interests at heart. At those times you need to know who you really are and what you stand for. Knowing when to take a stand for something (or when to compromise) can make you or break you. Trusting your intuition is an important aspect of decision-making.

The day our first batch of product was delivered proved the Laws of Attraction really work and I had proven how powerful this approach could be in business. I almost didn't believe it, except there it was, box after box of product right in front of me. I was at peace and thrilled by my team's accomplishment. Yet I was scared at the same time, for this was only the first step in the journey to have Integrity Cosmetics products in the world, make a difference in people's health and wellbeing, the environment, and philanthropy in the way I had envisioned. Now the real work begins, I thought.

My key points for success:

- Do energetic testing — it may surprise you and lead to time and cost savings. I wish I had done more in the months after we launched.

- Pick your team members carefully and believe in them as they are the experts; don't forget, as the business manager you retain overall responsibility.

- Believe in yourself, know who you really are and what you stand for, to see your dream be fulfilled.

Meet the Contributor

TRACEY THOMSON HOLDS a bachelor of business (marketing) from the Royal Melbourne Institute of Technology, Australia. She is happily married and lives with her husband, Mark, in Melbourne, Australia. Having worked for ten years in the telecommunications industry in Australia and the UK, Tracey has vast experience in product development and marketing in international markets. She was responsible for the 3G platform customer specification for T-Mobile in the UK and launching several new products to market.

Tracey's transition into the organic industry was born out of health issues and lifestyle changes she experienced, reinforced by the desire to make a difference on a large scale. Integrity Cosmetics organic skin care products are certified with the ACO (Australian Certified Organic), and use only the most pure, natural ingredients, absent of any harmful chemicals. The range is made in Australia, known for its high quality organic produce, and is cruelty free (free of testing on animals). A percentage of profits from every sale are contributed toward philanthropic projects leading to a more beautiful world. Tracey and Mark originally met at a ballroom dancing studio. Both were competitive dancers and are now embarking on the amazing and joyful journey of being parents.

Contact Tracey at www.integritycosmetics.com.au

Finding Passion after Success and Failure

Teresa Spencer (LBT #69)

Finding my path has been a journey that has taken over twenty-five years of exploration, learning, failure, and success.

When I was a teenager my father became a self-employed contractor and this was my first experience with an entrepreneur. I was in 4-H and Future Farmers of America; through my animal projects and the local fair I learned the importance of being exceptional so you received a higher return on your investment when selling your animals at the end of the season. My mother also introduced me to earning my own money through craft shows and selling handcrafted items, particularly during the holiday season.

Even though these were seasonal accomplishments, I learned that when you do things yourself you have control over how much money you can make. I've thought like an entrepreneur ever since. However, my own journey to success did not start until I was well into my twenties and it began because of a want, not a need or passion.

In 1985, I had my second child. My first entrepreneurial adventure was to provide daycare for children. I obtained the necessary state licenses to do this properly. I wanted to stay at home with my daughter, as I had missed those special moments with my first child, and I didn't want to repeat that mistake. Only one thing got in my way — I did not have a love for childcare as a business.

During this time I tried my hand with a multi-level marketing (MLM) company. I worked at the MLM in the evenings and weekends, while I spent my dawn-to-dusk hours on the daycare business, Monday through Friday. I worked both of these without business knowledge or the appropriate training. Because I did not focus on either business, these ventures ended after two years and I returned to a regular nine-to-five job.

In 1993 my husband lost his job and later that year, so did I. As both of us were unemployed, we started a company creating wooden yard signs. We did a few things correctly, had better success, and it lasted from 1993 to 1998. This business was not started without some challenges and struggle. We located used wood pieces for free from various sources to keep expenses down. Eventually we purchased wood for larger projects, were accepted to five consignment stores, and became regular attendees at local art festivals..

The business was started to feed our family; again, we had no formal business training or guidance, and it was sheer luck that it became successful. Eventually we closed the business when both of us returned to full-time jobs.

My current journey began in late 2004 — again, because of a want, not a need or passion. I wanted out of my current job. This began as my husband and I moved from the city to a rural area, a place where my passion and I reconnected after twenty-five years. I made inquiry calls for equine facilities and spoke to the salespeople about what they did, how they did it, and the average income in their field. The income and hours drew me to the direct sales industry, which at that point I had never done.

Once again I entered an industry without knowledge of the product, sales, or business training. Within the first three months after starting for a particular company, I received my first sale. I continued being a salesperson until I got tired of not being paid on time or being paid several months after a project was done. This is why California Horse Barns came to be. The formation of my own business allowed me to provide more services, information, and options for my clients. After five years of concentrating on sales, I stopped working leads and clients and stepped away from my business for a clarity break. I returned in late 2010 to an explosion of insight, knowledge, and vision for the future growth of my company. I now am not just a sales person for a company, but a consulting company for anyone who is purchasing equine facilities, large or small.

I joined Loral's Big Table with the intention of pursuing two other companies I had started in 2006 and 2009, but because they were not my passion I was not mentally connected to them. Those opportunities made me feel not authentic to myself. I was doing things that were expected of me to fit in with other women, rather than being and doing what I knew was right for me. Within 120 days of attending session one of Loral's Big Table I dropped both projects and came back to California Horse Barns and my passion.

I had major changes in how I look at business and where to get the answers. Sure, I was always resourceful in my career and found the answers I needed; but as an entrepreneur I was unable to do the same. I have since discovered it's not where you look, but how you look. When you look with your heart, become curious, and ask questions, people show up. Let me give you a few examples:

- Two weeks after my website was revised and went live, I received my first paying client.

- Less than one month after the website went live, I was offered a paid speaking engagement for the largest equine event in Southern California.

- As of this writing, I have had fifteen articles published locally in Southern California and nationally.

- I've written a book, *I Want to Build a Horse Barn — What to do First.*

- I am also responsible for the invention of two new equine safety ID products.

- I have successfully started a new company with a partner and friend.

This all happened less than eight months after the restart of California Horse Barns. I have also found it easier to locate the individuals and groups, organizations, and places where my target market hangs out. Before the restart I asked, "Where do I find these things and people?" Now I ask, "Who do I need to ask?" and the answer shows up.

Through discovering my passion for horses and enjoying the people I worked with to bring them their dream barns, I have started a second company called EquestriSafe, dedicated to equine safety. Its vision is to advance equine and equestrian protection and safety knowledge through education, research, and products. Through invention of products and finding a niche, others within the equine industry have noticed the company.

Some of my failures have been:

- Not asking the right questions
- Focusing on networking for the sake of networking
- Spending unnecessary money on things I thought I needed
- Not being authentic to myself
- Trying too hard to be perfect
- Thinking I can do it all on my own
- Not hiring the right coach
- Not taking criticism/ coaching well

Things I have succeeded at:

- Learning from mentors
- Asking questions
- Becoming involved
- Joining a mastermind group (or two or three)
- Paying for professional business coaching
- Learning that not all networking groups are for me

♦ Learning new ways of connecting with your target market

For me, riding horses with groups of people anytime I can is my way to network:

♦ Horse events

♦ Trade shows

♦ Becoming a sponsor for equine related events

My final thoughts are this:

♦ Be true to yourself.

♦ Find your passion and figure out how to pursue it.

♦ Have a support system of husband, family, kids, peers, coaches, or mentors.

♦ Keep track of the money.

♦ If networking doesn't work — try again until you figure it out.

♦ Don't be afraid to fail.

Meet the Contributor

TERESA SPENCER IS a passionate horse owner that has found a flare for business within the equestrian community. She has been a guest speaker at Equine Affaire in Southern California; published numerous articles for HorseCity.com and *Equestrian Trails Magazine*, as well as being involved in several equine related organizations. Her book, *How to Build a Horse Barn*, was published in 2011 and she has helped many families become proud owners of their dream barn. She continues her quest by building a company based on horse safety products.

Contact Teresa at www.californiahorsebarns.com or at her new business at www.EquestriSafe.com